MAKING LOVE WITH GOD

Books by Audrey Craft Davis

Metaphysical Techniques That Really Work
Making Love with God
Prosperity Consciousness
Metaphysical Encounters of a Fourth Kind

"The good I do is the rent that I pay
for the space I occupy on this planet."

Making Love with God

The Art of Mental Connection

Audrey Craft Davis,
Ms.D., Ps.D., D.D.

Blue Dolphin Publishing

Published by Blue Dolphin Publishing, Inc.
P.O. Box 8, Nevada City, CA 95959
Orders: 1-800-643-0765
Web: www.bluedolphinpublishing.com

ISBN: 978-1-57733-191-9

Library of Congress Cataloging-in-Publication Data

Davis, Audrey Craft.
Making love with God : the art of mental connection / Audrey Craft Davis.
p. cm.
ISBN-13: 978-1-57733-191-9 (pbk. : alk. paper)
1. Love. I. Title.

BF1045.L7D35 2006
204—dc22

2006030276

Cover design by James Craft.

Printed in the United States of America

10 9 8 7 6 5 4 3 2 1

Contents

Foreword

I have been a minister and teacher of metaphysics and spirituality for over twenty years and I have never read a book quite like this one. In *Making Love with God,* Dr. Audrey Craft Davis has given us another meaningful and wonderfully tender book.

It is said that you can feel people, even tell their quality by their vibrations. Perhaps Emerson had something of this sort in mind when he said, "What you are thunders so loud that I can't hear what you say." The general tone and quality of Audrey Craft Davis has since made itself known to me.

When I first met Audrey and her now departed husband Lou, I felt good. I remember thinking, "These are good people." And regardless of how the feeling came to me, it was correct. For after I came to know them, I knew they were good, also extremely witty—they were a very happy couple and treated each other (and everyone else they met) with a charming grace and understanding.

I recall thinking when Lou passed… "I hope Audrey can weather this storm." The loss of a loved one can be a numbing, debilitating, and shocking life experience. It is doubly so if the loss is sudden. Most people are unprepared for such a trauma and, as in all of life, none of us can know how we'll feel until we find ourselves there—alone, emotionally vulnerable, and afraid.

But Audrey not only pulled through, she again showed me that mourning is the by-product of love and she decided to share their love and pass on Lou's best qualities to all who cared to listen. Audrey has learned that when a person follows Universal Law, they cannot fail. She has set for herself a mark to be attained and has persevered until the day comes when she reaches her goal.

In this book Audrey has succeeded in demonstrating that after the grieving process ran its course, she found a way to help herself and others who have lost a mate by sharing her most intimate experiences.

Audrey explains in a beautiful and tender way how she and Lou brought God into their love life. When I asked her why she would want to share such an intimate experience with others, she said, "My main reason for writing this book is to help others take God into their love making." She went on to say, "Once you do, I promise you will never again leave God out of any part of your life, especially the part that deals with making love."

Audrey has shown to all those who have come in contact with her that each obstacle she has encountered has brought with it the opportunity to acquire the virtues needed to continue walking her path. She is proof that the death of a partner need not be the end of the relationship. She has shown that successfully moving on in life is not a matter of chance. For Audrey this success has come from preparation and meeting with opportunity. And for this, I thank her.

Rev. Dr. Paul F. Daniele, Ph.D., Th.D., D.D., P.C.
President Emeritus, The College of Metaphysical Studies
www.cms.edu

CHAPTER ONE

Making Love with God

We were caressing each other, which we often do as we snuggled into bed, when I made a rather startling suggestion to Lou, "Honey, God just gave me a different and wonderful idea. Want to hear it?"

"You bet I do," Lou answered, but he was a little shocked as I began, 'We are going to invite God to make love with us!"

"What? Do you mean what I think you mean?" He asked quizzically.

"Yes, I do mean just that." I answered.

"Honey, are you saying we are going to invite God into our sexual encounters?"

"Yes, sweetheart, that is exactly what I am saying."

"But won't that mean there will be three of us making love?"

"Well, since you and I are one since we got married and we have always been one with God, you could say the three of us are one."

"I thought that was what you were getting at. I am afraid you will have to take the initiative as I would not have the audacity or the knowledge of how to begin."

"The next time you get sexy, I'll take the lead. Okay?"

So, at the next crucial moment, I said to Lou. "Take my hand. We are going to pray."

"Sweetheart, are you sure God will be pleased with us praying in the midst of our sexual encounter? "

Disregarding his insinuation, I said, "Repeat after me. 'Dear Father- Mother God, since you know we do not want anything in our lives unless you can be part of it, we are inviting you to come and be a partner with us in our love experience. Thanks for understanding and becoming one with us at this most crucial moment. Amen."

Lou asks, "Now, what do we do?"

"We make love as we always have done."

Afterward, Lou was so exhilarated he couldn't believe what had just happened. "Look at me. I am not even winded, yet that is the most wonderful, exhilarating experience I have ever had! Our love life has been so terrific, I would never have thought of trying to improve it. But, as for this, all I can say is, 'Wow, now that is the way to make Love!"

So we continued for as long as Lou lived on this earth. Once you learn to invite God into every area of your life, and especially that very special place, you will never ever even think of going back to the way you originally made love.

This is where the title for this book "Making Love with God" came from: Why would I want to share such an intimate experience with you, the reader, especially since my husband is no longer here with me? My main reason for writing this book is to help others.

I hope that everyone who has a loving partner would learn to take God into their love-making. Once you do, I promise, you will never again leave God out of any part of your life, especially the most intimate part.

I am especially addressing wives with husbands who have heart problems and you are scared to death every time you make love, having learned that is when he is most vulnerable! There is no threat of any kind when you make love with God. My husband described it as so completely satisfying, one could never even imagine it … and ladies, absolutely no strain on his heart!

How does one make love with God? In addition to other chapters I want to elaborate on this most important area of our lives. I think I can best explain it by revealing mine and my husband's very own experience—thus the title of this book!

God meant for sex between man and woman to be the most beautiful, spiritual experience of all … one that would keep us all close to Him … and I might add that, if you will invite God into your sex life, it will indeed do all of that.

What "Tantra Yoga" was meant to teach...was that both partners are true children of God. But like so many beautiful spiritual experiences this has been misinterpreted many times. But from the beginning it was not so.

I talk to Lou a lot since he died. I was talking to him the other day, wondering why I had to have such crippling things happen to me the last few years before he died. I think I explain this very well further on. I had to use a wheelchair on our cruises.

He said to me, "Honey, if we could have traveled as we had done in the past, I would probably have died sooner and in some foreign country instead of in bed with you. I know we made a pact that neither one of us would ever leave this plane without the other. We found out that we do not have the last say in the matter, but really if I had to go first, I would have wanted to be by your side to the last moment, just the way I did. "

I still wonder why—after our five-hour trip into Heaven—I was healed and he wasn't. More about this as you get into the book.

I will hold in my heart forever his last words to me. This was after I had given him a thorough massage. He said, "I can feel the tremendous love in your wonderful hands. I have always loved your hands."

I answered, "Then let these hands you love so much bless that handsome face."

I caressed his face and his beard and kissed his eyes and his face and lips. He said, "Honey, I never thought I would ever know a great love like you."

I said, "You don't have a doubt, do you?"

His very last words to me were, "Not one!" I felt such contentment as I watched him snuggle down for a good night's sleep. I had no idea these would be his last words to me. He looked happy as he dosed off to sleep! At 4 AM he was gone!

I feel Lou's presence here at home with me and even while I was in deep grief. I realize that he can't take away that awful feeling of aloneness and absolute desertion, and I know that the grieving process must take its course.

And for those who have lost their husband as I have, after the grieving process has run its course, this will help you know that there is hope at the end of the tunnel ... that you can find a satisfying other experience and you can take God into this most intimate part of that relationship.

This book is also for you who still have mates; learn to take God into your sex life. If you feel this is a little too audacious, please keep reading. One point I want to make first to those who still have their mates: both of you just think, "what if we had had a fight or had rejected that 'good night kiss'—how would I be feeling now???"

Lou explained that now that he is an Angel, when I want him to help me, I must ask him, because Angels cannot usurp man's authority.

I have communicated with Lou (his name was Louis but I called him Lou) many times since his death. My daughter, Alice and I actually felt him standing with us at the mortuary as we viewed the body, and we knew he came home with us. That body we left at the graveside was not him.

He loved and believed so much in my work and loved me so much.... I believe he actually made an agreement with God to give up his life in exchange for my daughter, Alice's.

Why do I believe this? Because he felt that if my daughter could be healed of that awful heart condition, she would always be there for me. Since he was a good bit older than me and she was still young, she would be around much longer than he would. He loved helping me in any way he could. I was proud that he told me that I was the only person on earth who had made him feel important. He often told me he felt that was why he was brought into my life ... to help me fulfill my purpose on Earth.

Later on in the book I give a detailed account of this. Later I tell how Lou made an agreement with God that if He would heal my daughter's very serious heart condition, he, Lou would be willing to go on to Heaven in exchange. We both know that is exactly what he did. It happened when my husband and I went to the Benny Hinn Healing Crusade.

My husband, Lou had only met my daughter once. So after his death when she came to comfort me, it was strange that Lou came to her and she saw him vividly 13 different times—yet I have not seen him. I feel his presence and I communicate with him telepathically. She saw him plainly as he came to her through my hologram of Jesus when she visited me after his death. He chose her as a channel.

Since my husband's death, Alice gets clear messages concerning anything that might affect me in any way. She will be told when to get someone out of my life. This happened several times. She is guided as to when I should take a certain action on my own behalf or to let me know when I am in harm's way. This continues to this day. She knew from the beginning that these messages were from my husband. She has become my confidant and advisor, and she knows it all comes from my husband who is in heaven.

For instance recently she called from Ohio and told me that there is a giant dead tree in my yard that must be cut down. I have so many large trees in my yard, I had not even noticed it. I had a tree specialist come and examine the tree. He confirmed her message. The tree had been hit by lightning during our series of hurricanes. So I had it brought down. A couple of months later she got the same message again. I again had the tree examined which was a prime example of the first, a giant pine tree. It also had to come down. All of these messages are from my deceased husband.

Alice says Lou keeps her informed when I need anything or need to be aware of a specific move. Many such miracles have come about since his death.

The body we left at that gravesite was just the house God loaned him. I know of many people who go to the graveside to talk and commune with a deceased loved one. Of course, if you feel that way, then go, by all means. One dear friend goes to his wife's grave almost every week to talk to her ... and George Burns went to his wife Gracie's gravesite every day to commune with her. And I don't doubt that these people do commune with their loved ones this way, but the point I want to make is that the deceased one is only there because their dear one is there. They are not in that grave.

I remember when before his death Lou insisted that we go to Georgia to his Mother's gravesite and of course I went. I told him that the only reason she would be there was because that was where she had to go to meet him. And when we got there, she was not in the grave. We clearly knew exactly where she was. She was near the beautiful trees which line the graveyard. But I am happy we went, for Lou would not have known she was not in that grave if he hadn't had that experience.

No matter what has happened we must have something to look forward to; something to hope for. Someone said, "Man can live for many months without food, a few weeks without water and three minutes without air, but he cannot live one minute without hope."

It just didn't seem fair that Lou would die. One of the things I think my husband and I were most thankful for was that we had each found someone to love and grow old with. We didn't mind getting older because we felt the years are worth the lessons we glean from them.

As my oldest sister said when she became age eighty, it is the best age she has experienced yet, and she would not want to be any other age. That gave me something to look forward to. And then I came upon this message: "'The Day out of Time' beginning of the New Golden Age 9/6/04 was prophesied many thousands of years ago. Our vibrations are being increased because Ascension is upon us! But that process did not stop in 2004. It goes on and on till we reach our Ascension in 2005; and after that 'til 2012 and then forever."

Since my husband died, I dreaded having to grow old alone. I did not want to live any longer.

So I decided that I would no longer do all this "health stuff," with special foods, certain exercises, vitamins and minerals—none of this anymore. I really did all this mostly because my husband was a good bit older than me and I did it mostly for him. I felt that with my good care he would live a long life.

And he did. When we got married he had only a few months to live. We had twenty-three beautiful years together.

So I reasoned that without all this health stuff, I could leave this planet sooner and be with Lou. But when I shared this with my daughter she stopped me dead in my tracks.

She asked me, "Mom, what could be worse than growing old alone?" I answered immediately, "Nothing."

She came back with, "Oh, yes there is something worse ... being sick and growing old alone." That really brought me to my senses. I got back to my healthy regime. Much later I found this:

> Milk every moment for all the pleasure you can get from it. When you say, "It is my dominant intent to look for things that feel good today. No matter where I'm going, no matter what I'm doing, no matter who I'm doing it with, it is my dominant intent to look for what I'm wanting to see, to look for things that feel good," and the more you develop the habit of that kind of vibration—the more the Universe understands that that's who you are! And so the more you have access to those kinds of things!"

Sometimes we must look for a better way and we become aware that the universe is just waiting for us to make known what it is we want. In so many experiences, we are limited only by our imagination. I'll give you another example of how powerful your God-mind is. I searched for something to make me smile more and I remembered this past experience:

CHAPTER TWO

Sex in Absentia

My husband had to be out of town for a week. After an absence of several days, he called me and explained how much he needed me. So, I said, "Okay, I'll come to you."

He answered, "Oh, no darling, don't fly up here. I will be home in a few days."

"Oh, I'm not going that route. Since you are already in bed as you always are when you call me, just put your arm out and I will be with you."

He exclaimed, "Honey, don't kid around at a time like this."

"Oh, I'm not kidding around, believe me. In the morning when you awaken you will try to imagine how such a dream can be so real, but remember I'm telling you right now, we will make love tonight."

The following morning my husband called and was absolutely flabbergasted. He said, "I would say that I just had a most fantastic dream; but you told me last night to expect an unbelievably powerful love session. So, it had to be the real thing. I don't understand it, but all I can say is, 'Wow.'"

"As a man believeth in his heart, so is it." How much can you believe?

I know of other couples who experience sexual gratification in this manner when they must be apart. We are truly limited only by our lack of imagination and belief.

One thing that hampers most people when they think of sex: they really believe that this body is what we are. Not so—we are spirit—not body. Once you let this sink in real good, you will have no problem believing the following.

CHAPTER THREE

The Art of Mental Connection

The "Art of Mental Connection" concerns that magical ingredient that exists between two people who are really in love. It is so very under-evaluated. Why? I believe it is because so often we cannot stretch the imagination to realize the magnitude of the mind. If we knew how powerful our mind is, it would scare us to death! In our world, everything is whatever we think it is! I have said so often, "If you think your world is lined with rainbows, it is; and if you think your world stinks, it does!"

Our only mental limitation IS whatever we think it is. Why is this any harder to believe than some happenings that we experience on a regular basis? For example, who hasn't had the experience of thinking of a particular person, only to have that very one call immediately and often they will say, "I don't even know why I called." Of course it was a mental connection.

Nothing can happen until someone thinks about it. If you can think it, you can do it! This includes the sex act. Sex is 95% mental ... 5% physical action. Think about that! If you hadn't thought about it ... it could never happen. The majority of people think that the sex act only involves two bodies. The physical portion, I repeat, amounts to only 5%.

The important part, that magical contact, is initiated in the pineal gland which is located in the center of the head ... yes, 95%... is actually your God Consciousness! Now do you see why I tell you that God originally intended the sex act to be the most spiritual, beautiful, Godly act human beings could experience. When in this 95% God-consciousness state, you cannot even think a bad thought.

Whether in the imagination or in actual contact, I want to show how this exercise can actually be so complete between two people (at a distance) that a climax can be initiated as surely as if their two bodies were actually connected. How...by just using the imaginative power of their two collective minds and it will always originate in the pineal gland which is located in the center of the head.

This is where the spiritual part of you resides. It is the spiritual body that is involved. 95% of the entire sexual encounter, whether physical or spiritual, had to begin in the pineal gland or it could never happen. It is your spiritual body which is involved in either type of connection; once again proving that we are spirit, not body. Nothing can ever be physical until it has evolved in the mental realm. I repeat, "Nothing can happen until someone thinks about it!"

Remember the great Doctor of the Senate, Peter Marshall? His wife wrote about how, when she so desperately needed him, her deceased husband would come and make love to her.

I am sharing some of our most intimate experiences in hopes of touching those who have lost a loved one. I want to show those who are suffering from grief that the loved one who is no longer with you physically is still there as much as ever in spirit. The real person is invisible and has always been invisible, even when he or she was here in the physical; yes, even when he or she lived here on earth and was your companion.

We are all invisible, for we are spirit. What you see with your physical eyes is the house the person resides in. We are not a body enclosing a spirit. We are a spirit inhabiting a body. In other words, we are not a physical being having a spiritual experience; we are a spirit having a physical experience.

And just think, since that person has gone ahead of us into heaven, we now have our very own private Guardian Angel. If you ever doubted the existence of angels, you have no need to doubt any more. The body which we cherish is not the person. That person you adored is now an Angel, a spirit. He is with you, just as much as ever. You just cannot touch or see him.

I appreciate so very much being able to tune into my husband's spirit. That is how I was able to receive his message that he is now my Guardian Angel and how he could tell me that he was giving me a new car for "HIS Birthday."

LOU BOUGHT ME A NEW CAR FOR *HIS* BIRTHDAY.

Lou's birthday would have been September 17th but he died on the 4th as we were planning his birthday celebration, our 80th cruise and another trip to Hawaii. He is still here in the house with me. I don't see him but I get his messages loud and clear. He communicates through my daughter, Alice. She has experienced many psychic gifts since childhood. She is a wonderful channel.

Lou has appeared right here in my house to several of my psychic friends and to my daughter, Alice, many times. I haven't seen him because when I think of him, the sadness tosses me back into my 5% beta consciousness. But I feel his presence very often and I receive his messages clearly. A good example was when Lou bought me a new car for **HIS** birthday.

I had given up driving years before, and we bought a new larger van just five months before he died. I never thought I would give up my driving for anyone.

But Lou and I had great plans and the only way we could fulfill them—and me still have time for writing my books and magazine articles—was for me not only to give up my driving but also relinquish many of the chores around the house which Lou eagerly took over. He really cherished my books and all my writing so much he did not want anything to interfere with that in any way.

He believed that helping me was his reason for being on Planet Earth. I was so proud when he told me that I was the only person who had ever made him feel important!

He convinced me that if I would do it his way, I could get my writing done and we could still travel around the world and cruise as often as we wished and fulfill our dreams together. We did just that.

We visited many countries, and took seventy-nine cruises. I did some of my writing and seminars while aboard ships. He loved helping me. He believed so much in me and my writing, that when we first met, he would carry a small recorder in his shirt pocket. He would then ask me many questions as we danced, usually about metaphysics. Then he would take them off the recorder and type up the information.

From the time we met he began telling me that I must put that precious knowledge into books. At that time I put it into seminars, teaching and counseling. If it weren't for him, I doubt that my books would have made it into print.

Soon after his death, I heard him say, "Honey, you can't drive that big van. You must have a very secure smaller car. I will set it up for you." I will keep reminding you; our communication was and still is via telepathy, as are all our conversations since his death.

To this day Helen and Holmes are flabbergasted at what Lou did and the way he brought it about. He told me to call Helen and tell her that my deceased husband had chosen Holmes, her husband who was a car salesman, to bring just the right car to me ... not to worry he (Lou) would make sure that Holmes brought the perfect car for me. What was very strange about this was that Lou had never met Helen's husband and he had only met Helen once or twice.

Lou said to me, "You are going to be so excited over this car, that when you put your hands on the steering wheel, you will shout, "Oh my God, this is my car!"

I answered, "Darling, I wouldn't be that excited if you gave me a new car loaded with million dollar bills. Nothing is worthwhile without you!"

But I did as Lou told me and called Helen and gave her the message. To this day they are both still dumbfounded as to how Holmes, Helen's husband knew what car to bring. Holmes is still confused as to why he brought the car that he did.

I knew when he drove up in a red Mercury Sable that was not my car. Lou knew I would never buy a red car. I found later, Lou chose the red color for effect. I wasn't even going to go out and look at that car. But Holmes said, "I brought it all the way from Clearwater. Surely you will at least take it for a drive."

I thought, "OK, to please him, I'll take it for a drive. But I know that is not my car."

I walk out; Holmes opened the door, I got in and sat down while Holmes got in on the other side. I felt nothing as I strapped myself in, but as I put my hands on the steering wheel, I heard myself shout, "Oh, my God, this is my car!"

Then I exclaimed, "Lou told me I was going to do that!"

That car was delivered to me on Lou's birthday...every paper signed, license in place, ready to drive and Lou said, "It will always be filled with angels just for you, darling." Lou had bought me a new car not for my birthday but **for his**!

One point I want to make here is that your husband or wife, even if they suffered from jealousy (which my husband did) without reason, in heaven they do not know such emotion. All they want is for you to be happy. I know of several cases where the deceased loved one has or is actually helping to find a good mate for the one left behind.

I reiterate: you cannot think without seeing a picture. Think of your loved one right now. Can't you see him or her? ... actually see how they smile or laugh, or see that funny little quirk that is so familiar to you? Your loved one is very much alive. You have seen him, touched him, lived with him and loved him or her.

Just as our body does not belong to us, so the body of your loved one never did belong to him or her. It was just a house God loaned them for a short time. That is why God tells us that our body is "His Temple." It doesn't even belong to us.

So when a person leaves the body, he or she is at home with God. But he or she is more alive than ever. It is just that he is in spirit form. The reason we cannot see him or her is that their vibrations have been raised to a much higher rate than our own. To see something or someone you must possess the same rate of vibration; which is why clairvoyant ones can see one who has passed on. The seer must go into a trance state which raises their vibrations, just as my dear friend Joanne did when she saw my deceased husband in my living room.

If you think you are receiving messages from a departed loved one, all you have to do to prove it is to pay attention to the first thought. That will be your loved one. If you listen to the second or the third, it is not your beloved. Why? By the time you have had a second thought, your beta brain waves (that 5% of your brain) have kicked it and those vibrations are much too low to be coming from the deceased one.

The best time to communicate with a deceased one or even an Angel is when just dozing off or first awakening. At this time you are in your alpha or theta brain wave frequency. As we sleep we dwell in our higher consciousness. This means that our vibrations are much higher, resulting in the ability to see those on the other side, even Angels. As we are growing limp just prior to sleep, we are in our alpha or theta brain wave frequency (that 75 to 95 % of your brain).

We alternate from one frequency to another during sleep. Just prior to sleep is a good time to contact Angels or deceased loved ones. Our vibrations are much higher and closer to the rate of those dear ones.

I must tell you how Lou got to know his Archangel, Uriel. He would awaken out of a sound sleep fighting, flailing his arms and shouting! I asked why he kept doing that. Lou told me that every so often this huge figure would awaken him; that he was so big, he was frightening! I suggested that the next time that happened, to let me talk to him.

Lou would see him because as I have explained, he would be sleeping when Uriel appeared, so he was in a higher brain wave frequency of 75 to 95%.

By the time he made all that noise and awakened me so suddenly, I would be in my little beta 5% consciousness and could not see him.

In our work-a-day world our vibrations are too low to make contact.

So I did not see Lou's Archangel but I sensed his presence. I began to talk to Uriel. I asked him how long he had been trying to get in touch with Lou. He said he had been trying to contact him for eight years. He just wanted Lou to accept him so he could be around to help him.

You might ask how I knew it was Uriel? Each sign has its own Archangel. Lou is a Virgo so his Archangel had to be Uriel. My Archangel is Raphael because my sign is Gemini.

I went right out and bought Lou an Angel figure and we named him Uriel. I placed it on the table beside his favorite chair. I told Lou to talk to his Archangel Uriel and ask him for help whenever he needed to make a decision. I knew that this little Angel figure would remind him to seek Uriel's advice. I explained that talking to Angels and Archangels raises our vibrations and helps prepare us for ascension.

The reason a psychic person can see or hear those on the other side is that she or he slips into a trance-like state: the alpha or theta brain wave frequency which is of that higher vibration and operates at 75% to 95% of brain wave capacity.

This is why we usually do not physically see our Angels. Their vibrations are so much higher than our own. If the Angels would slow down their vibrations or if we could speed up our own, we could see them. I have not seen my late husband although I feel his presence and I hear him telepathically talking to me.

When on occasion, we do see Angels, spirit beings or deceased loved ones, there has had to be a change in vibrations. I will give you an example of being automatically in the theta brain wave frequency, which is normal for sleep—we drift back and forth from alpha to theta all night. This can happen as a result of a car accident when one has left the body. I awakened but was still in my higher frequency when I sensed a presence in the room. I lifted myself up on my elbow and there beside my bed stood a beautiful little Angel. I nudged my husband and told him to take a look.

He looked and then he said, "That's nice," and went right back to sleep. The reason we could see the Angel was because we were still in that natural state of alpha or theta, which speeds up one's vibrations. It turned out to be my "Joy Guide, Giva."

I have not seen Lou here in my house, probably because every time I even think of him, my grief tosses me into my beta consciousness; that 5% brain wave could never see an Angel.

But my daughter saw him right here thirteen times. She can think of Lou without grieving since she had only seen him once which allows her to be in her higher consciousness.

Also, my friend, Joanne who was sitting on the couch visiting with me when she suddenly went into a trance-like state, which is why a psychic can see things others do not see. She said, "Lou was buried in a blue suit with a vest and turtleneck shirt."

"How could you know that?" I asked.

She answered, "He is standing right here in your living room."

The higher vibration into which Joanne entered (the theta brain wave frequency) had to be the same as Lou's, which is what made him visible to her. To actually see one who has passed over, one's vibrations must be equal to that of the deceased.

Angels come in every size and likeness and most often as human beings. Remember in the Bible where the scripture reveals to Abraham and Sarah that they were entertaining "Angels unaware." These Angels looked just like humans. Lou and I have experienced this several times. I wonder how many times you or I have played the part of an Angel without our knowledge.

We are channels through which God's power can flow. Some of us may be better channels, perhaps because of our awareness that it is possible, or it could be because of incidents in our lives, which have made believers of us.

I find that often when we encounter someone who doubts the power of this precious energy, it is because that person has never had an experience of what we call the "supernatural."

I feel blessed that I have been chosen to be a channel of this energy. God has allowed me to be an instrument for His Healing energy many times for which I am very grateful. I am not always sure of the route the special power might take. The healing energy may come through my hands, my eyes and sometimes through meditation and visualization through what we refer to as "absentia," absent healing, meaning the person who is being healed is not present.

I prefer this type of healing. This is often the most effective as it eliminates the possibility of the patient's possible doubting, as noted in the chapter on "Healing in absentia."

Of course if the person being healed can join a deep faith with the healer's, it can strengthen the healing. One point I'd like to make: Before doing a healing of any kind, it is good to put a protective light around yourself and, after the healing, visualize yourself standing under a cleansing shower ... to make sure no negative residue remains.

Once I did a healing for a friend's feet without her knowledge, I thought. But the next time I saw her she told me how her feet didn't hurt any more and that she knew the healing came through me. I asked her how she knew it was from me. She said that as she felt the Healing Angel energy, there was not a doubt as to where it was coming from. Often God will borrow a human body for an Angel to use to get the job done.

If there is anything great in any of us, it is the creative force expressing through us. The divine mind's nature is to create. Most great artists admit that there is an unseen creative principle which works through them to accomplish their feats of genius. So, you see why it is so easy for me to believe in this tremendous potential.

SPIRIT RELEASEMENT FOR INANIMATE AS WELL AS ANIMATE OBJECTS

Psychotronics explains how molecular electronics has the capacity to heal physical ills by using a holographic image of the drug instead of the drug. We think in holograms—for example, cancer patients: the cancer is seen as being eaten up by the fighter cells. If man can think it, he can do it!

I thought to myself, "I need to write an article concerning spirit releasement therapy for entities that abide in inanimate objects like computers." My computer was possessed. It had somehow acquired a demon, a Trojan virus, and it was giving me fits. I was mulling this idea over in my mind as my friend, Dee, arrived.

Still in deep thought, I said to Dee, "Everything has life, spirit. Nothing is dead. I feel that God is giving me a very special message about how to heal inanimate objects. It might sound very strange at first but I really believe it is possible to heal remote things. I think I could do a de-possession or spirit releasement for my computer. Nothing is dead. Everything has life. So why not heal an inanimate object. Dr. Wickland of the early 19th-century worked with spirit obsession and possession of people. He believed that all illness was caused by a demon or spirit possession. Since life abides in all things that has to include inanimate things," I mused.

I had used this therapy many times for humans, but this was the first time I had ever thought of doing it for an inanimate object. I just felt that the message which kept running through my head was no accidental thought. It kept thundering through my mind, "Everything is alive. Nothing is dead!"

The thought hung in there. "Am I out of my mind, or am I receiving a very special message?... I must find out! I'll lead the way," I said to Dee.

I was feeling my way as we put our hands on my computer and then actually visualized ourselves leading those spirits (demons) out of my computer, and placing their hand into the hand of Jesus, just as I always would do if they were human beings. Next, we did a cleansing and then a complete healing and placed protection around my computer, just as we would do for a human being. I worked the same way as I had done for humans, and why not? I repeat, "Everything has life! And if it has life, it must have a spirit. Nothing is dead!"

Remember the statement, "Whatever man can conceive and believe, he can achieve." Jesus said it a little differently, "As is your faith or (as you believe), so be it unto you."

I'm so thankful that now I know that this process works for inanimate things as well as animate. It worked just like it has with human beings, and it has been proven the many times I have taught this process to others. It has never failed. Why? It worked because we as human beings are not doing it. God is doing the work. We use our minds as instruments.

I've been doing this releasing for people for many years now. I'll relate a real case, not using the person's name. Martha's friend shook so violently and incessantly that she had to be kept in the hospital under special care. The doctors and specialists were unable to stop this violent shaking. I told my friend that I knew a process that had never failed that I believed would work for her friend. But I said. "I want you to do the work, so you can prove it to yourself."

Martha is very good at helping others. And I wanted to put this procedure to the test by someone who knew nothing about the treatment and also for a very severe test, to prove to myself it never fails.

So I led Martha and she did the actual spirit releasement. When she finished, she called the hospital and her friend had suddenly stopped shaking and was released immediately from the hospital.

I helped Dee to familiarize herself with "Spirit Releasement Therapy." I learned it from Dr. William Baldwin's book of the same name. Not long after purchasing and studying the book, I had to call on him to help me do my first "spirit releasement" for a loved one. It proved so successful that I have continued the process whenever needed.

Jesus cast out many demons (spirits) as reported in the Bible. So often a person assumes that when the Bible speaks of demons, it is referring to really "bad" entities. This is not always so. Demon can mean "spirit," and it can be the spirit of a very lovely or dear deceased person who suffered a violent death and was so shaken up by it that he or she jumped into the first open aura he could find.

One particular time a friend called me to please come help her friend. "What is the problem?" I asked.

She said she just did not understand what had happened to her friend. She related how that suddenly he went from being a very light smoker to, as she related, "smoking like a chimney." He seemed possessed with the habit all of a sudden.

I asked if someone close to him had suddenly died in a violent accident. She answered yes, that a good friend had very recently been killed in an auto accident.

"Was the deceased a heavy smoker?" I asked.

"Well, yes, but how could you know that?" she asked.

I answered, "I'll explain when I get there."

I did a spirit releasement for her friend, Frank. He is fine and no longer a heavy smoker. I explained that the spirit of his friend, who was very frightened and confused at the time of death, had jumped into Frank's aura, which had to be open at the time. This happens because the one who is killed violently is often so stunned he loses his way, which normally would be to just drift on into the light.

I have read of cases where a person is pinned inside a car and the spirit which moves out temporarily sits in mid-air or alongside and watches as his own body is being extricated from a wrecked car, with no sensation whatsoever. The reason this is different is that the person involved is probably knocked unconscious or is in a coma at the time of the crash and does not feel the trauma ... and it is not that one's time to die.

To release an inhabiting spirit one literally leads the (demon) spirit into the light. One point I would like to make is that this is much better than sending the spirit into shock, which leaves that spirit free to roam about getting into other people's auras. Earlier in this article, I mentioned Dr. Carl Wickland who, in the early 1900s, was also an exorcist, and he dealt with spirit obsession and possession. If necessary, he would use electrical shock to drive out the possessing spirit, but he preferred to lead the spirit into the light. This way there is one less demon (spirit) for the world to have to deal with. He would use an electrical shock if necessary to release the spirit, but this way, as he explained, that spirit is free to attach to someone else. When led into the light the spirit is blessed and no longer a burden.

The person is not the patient. The spirit, not the body, is the patient. When I do a spirit releasement, I literally see (visualize) the figure of Christ (you might see your special spirit guide or angel) as He comes to meet us, and I place the hand of the demon into His hand. Jesus then leads that spirit (demon) into the light where it can never disturb anyone ever again.

Then the one who has been released must have a thorough cleansing. I do this by seeing a cleansing light as it flows through that one. Then I visualize the person completely filled with light ... that the light actually spurts out the top of the head and overflows around the body, forming a halo of light. Next, I ask my angel to cleanse the person's aura, wrap it around the person, and seal it, so nothing but light can enter.

The large group of doctors who formed this Spirit Releasement Therapy Group say that everyone should do a spirit releasement for themselves and their loved ones twice a week. This might sound like a lengthy procedure, but actually it can be done in very short order. When one realizes that he or she is only an instrument, and that God is the one who does the actual work, it is not difficult and can be done in minutes. What seems astounding to me is that it never fails and can be done in a very few minutes.

You might ask, "Where or how does one pick up these spirits (demons)?" These demons hang around places like bars, hospitals, gravesites, anywhere there is misery. If you happen to have a weak spot in your aura, they can get in. How do you get a weak spot in the aura? This can happen as a result of being overly tired or ill, or in cases of grief or stress. One should place a white light protection around himself and his or her loved ones every time you go outside your home. And hopefully leave that place cleansed the same way with a protective light around the house and your automobile.

After doing spirit releasement for another, you should visualize yourself standing under a shower of light as a cleansing. Go through this procedure once you have read this article and notice that it took only a very few minutes ... and it works every time. You can do this for a disturbed pet also.

CHAPTER FOUR

Angels Appear As Human

Did you know that Angels can borrow a human body to perform miracles, and the person usually is not aware that their body is involved? This has probably happened many times in all our lives but I was made aware of this three times ... once when it was decided that a huge tree in front of my house must be cut down. It was on city property but they needed my permission to dispose of it.

Since I revere all life and a tree is life, I told my Angel that I did not want to make such a decision. So I was not surprised when a man rang my door bell and informed me he was here to make a decision concerning the tree. I invited him in as he handed me his business card.

He was tall and as I looked up into his eyes, I said, "When I look into your eyes, I can think of nothing but God!" All he answered was, "Yea."

This time I deliberately looked deeply into his eyes and repeated my statement and again all he answered was, "Yea."

He told us that he had come to make the decision about the tree and that he had decided; the tree must come down.

The next day I needed to talk to him about the tree decision. I told him that I was the woman who owned the house in Oldsmar where he had been the day before to make the decision about the tree in front of my house.

He seemed totally surprised as though he had no idea of what I spoke. I read off his name on his card and asked if that was his card to which he answered, "Yes."

"Is this your name, address and phone number?" I asked. He again answered, "Yes."

I again repeated that he had been at my house the day before and furthermore that he had handed me his business card when he was here. He sounded completely surprised as he denied it and replied, "I have not been in Oldsmar for fifteen years and I don't know what you are talking about!"

Then suddenly I remembered Abraham and Sarah's experience as reported in the Bible and I concluded, just like them, I had just entertained an Angel unawares.

I remembered other instances where this had happened. An Angel had obviously borrowed the man's body and he didn't even know it. Then it made sense to me why I thought of God when I looked at him.

Another incident that left my husband and me breathless was when we had run an ad to sell our large double-sided refrigerator which we had just replaced. We had it placed outside on the patio.

In a day or two a truck pulled up and the driver seemed interested in the refrigerator. He wandered over and told us he had no money but that he would be happy to haul away the refrigerator for us. We assumed he meant that he would come back because he was alone and the bed of the truck was very high and had no drop-down back to it.

We agreed and told him that he could pay us when he got the money. We nearly fainted as he walked over to that huge refrigerator, picked it up and lifted it onto that truck bed which was as high as he was tall. We still cannot imagine how he could have lifted that refrigerator. There is no way he could reach around it even if he could pick it up. As we stood there with our mouths open, he drove away! That had to be an Angel!

Then there was the incident where it had to be an Angel encounter. My husband and I had just installed a new mail box. We had some concrete mix left and we did not want to waste it. I said, "If we had some sand, we could repair those steps."

I had no sooner made that statement until a truck pulled up in front of our house. The man stuck his head out the window and asked, "I don't suppose you people could use some sand could you? I had some left from my last job and I don't want to go all the way back to the supply yard to dump it."

Of course we answered in the affirmative and then just looked at each other. We had to laugh! Of all the places in Pinellas County, how did he know that we needed some sand? Another of God's Angels ... wow!

CHAPTER FIVE

Miracle Vase

I must tell you about my "Miracle Vase." If you have ever seen one of these huge Mexican vases like the one that stands in my dining room, you will know why I am delighted to tell you about this miracle. Here is how it happened:

My husband and I drove our motor home from Florida to Texas with plans to cross over the foot-bridge into Mexico. At that time one could find some real bargains in Mexico. So when we arrived, we parked our motor home in Texas at a motor home park.

One did not dare take a vehicle of any kind into Mexico. There would have been nothing left of it within five minutes.

We walked over the foot-bridge and found a lot of bargains as we expected, but the prize that I wanted more than all the rest was too big and heavy to carry across the foot-bridge. Oh how I desired one of those huge vases!

As we arrived back at our Motor Home, I said, "I have always gotten anything I really desired. I don't understand why I did not get one of those beautiful vases. I really want one of them."

My hubby answered, "There must be an exception to all rules."

So I gave up on the idea and the last day some of the ladies of the motor home park decided to walk into town though it was miles away. What else was there to do?

We had walked what seemed like miles and was in sight of the town area when I saw one of those huge vases lying outside of a small business.

I lost all interest in the stroll with the others and wandered over to that business. The owner saw that I was obviously interested in the vase he had thrown out.

"What are you going to do with that huge vase?" I asked.

He informed me that it had a chip out of the very top and he was putting it in the trash. Then he said, "If you are interested in it, give me five bucks and it is yours."

I quickly reached into my purse and pulled out a five dollar bill. He took it and disappeared back inside. I stood there wondering how I was going to get that big, oversized vase back to our motor home. It was miles away? I knew my husband would not even think of disconnecting all those camper electric and fuel lines just to drive that distance to pick up a vase, no matter how much I liked it.

Out of nowhere there appears a very muscular gentleman. He says, "Looks like you can use some help," and walks over to the huge vase; hoists it upon his shoulder and heads in the direction of our motor home park. I ran after him exclaiming,

"Hey, you can't imagine how far you will have to carry that heavy thing!"

He quipped, "Good for my muscles!" and just kept going. He never once asked where I lived. He took it straight to our very motor home and unloaded it inside. I turned around to pay him but he had vanished! He had to be an Angel!

This same Angel appeared again, years later. We had moved into my big twelve-room, two-story house. We were enjoying decorating and purchasing new things for it. We went shopping because we had in mind a certain size and style bar for the upstairs Florida room. Finally we came across just the right one. As we stood admiring it, the salesman came over.

"I see you like that bar. Shall I have it loaded into your vehicle for you?"

We agreed, paid him and headed out with our treasure. As we arrived home and walked around to the back of our van, we found we could not budge any part of that heavy bar. We were so pleased with it we had not noticed it was made of pressed wood which is terribly heavy! As we stood there perplexed, we heard a familiar voice which we remembered, "Looks like you can use some help!"

Wow, there stood that same muscular guy we had encountered in Texas! Before we could say a word, he picked that thing up.

I yelled. "That heavy bar is for upstairs and all the way to the back."

He responded, "Good for my muscles!"

Then he said to my husband, "You just guide the rear end," and headed upstairs with that heavy thing! He took it right to the spot which was in the far end of the upstairs, unloaded it in the Florida Room right where we wanted it placed, and headed downstairs.

We followed close behind. Wow, as I started to ask how much we owed him, that Angel disappeared ... again!

Are you beginning to understand why almost nothing surprises me any more? This is why many years ago with so many miracles happening, I became really serious as I stated, "I know you are God, but if you are going to continue with all these miracles, I have to say, 'Please don't send me another miracle unless you give me a witness. I do not want to doubt my own mind, nor do I want others to question it!'"

From that time to the present, I have had a witness to every miracle and there has been a myriad of them.

I want to insert this bit of information concerning Angels that may not be your idea of an Angel. Have you ever been in a store or business and seen a dear one who is either mentally or physically impaired so badly that all you can think of is pity? Be reverent when around such a one. That person probably took on that position before he or she was ever born.

"But why," you might ask "would a person choose such a life?" It was probably to be able to move higher much faster than usual in a particular lifetime. And many times that burden becomes more than the person can endure. In such a case an Angel will often move into that disabled mind and body to allow that dear soul to be free to go on to his or her reward and will live out that lifetime in their place. So, be careful when seeing such a one, you may be observing an Angel.

CHAPTER SIX

Do Animals Go to Heaven?

Back to Angels and how they can appear in many different shapes and sizes:

How often we hear, "Do animals, especially dogs and cats, go to Heaven? And can they take on the form of an Angel?"

I would answer "Yes" to both questions. I will give you a prime example. My daughter Alice's little poodle was what is considered "old age" for a dog when cancer struck his frail body. She knew she should, as they say, "have him put to sleep," but she just couldn't! So, she sat by his bed every moment she could with her hand caressing him. If she ventured away to attend to some chore, he would cry pitifully until he could feel her hand again.

As it became closer to the time for him to leave this world, she sat day and night with her hand constantly soothing him. She relayed to me that as he died, though her hand was still on his body, as he breathed his last breath, he arose out of his doggie bed and went bounding down the hall like the puppy he had been when they first brought him home! This should comfort all of you who have wondered, "Do dogs go to Heaven?"

Animals know about Angels. Here is a prime example. I once lived beside a neighbor who believed that, to train a dog to be a watch dog, you must be cruel to him to make him a mean, angry dog.

One day when the sun was at its hottest, I noticed that my neighbor's dog was tied to a short leash and he was panting like each breath would be his last.

My heart went out to him as I placed my hands together and looking toward heaven, I asked God to please send an Angel to help that dog. As I watched, immediately that dog sighed and lay down with his head on his paws and he looked like he was in seventh heaven! Visibly nothing had changed, but he was oblivious to the hot sun and the short leash.

From that day on, that dog loved me. To everyone but me he had become that vicious animal that barked at everyone who passed on the sidewalk or came near the fence. But I could walk up to the fence and he would sit down and begin trying to talk to me. His mouth would be going a mile a minute. I would say to him, "You know I summoned an Angel for you, don't you?" Oh, he let me know that he knew all right!

I will repeat the following statement several times in this book, "You must ask an Angel when you wish them to do something. God created Angels to serve man and they cannot usurp man's authority."

TRIXIE

Angels often work with animals and they can even take the form of an animal. A good example of this was my children's dog, Trixie. She was my children's guardian Angel as they were growing up.

We had a raspberry patch and my children loved to pick the berries. Trixie watched over them closely. If either Alice or Jim went near that garden, she would get between them and the raspberry patch. She would not let them take a step until she had gone through every single row. When she was sure it was safe, she would go over and sit down.

Once she got bitten by a poisonous snake. My husband took a bottle of turpentine and turned it up over the wound. It was amazing to watch that turpentine turn green in color as the poison was pulled out of the bite.

My husband learned in no uncertain terms that Trixie was an Angel in disguise. He was most proud of his thoroughbred hunting dogs. Seemingly forgetting the guardian she had been to our two children, he decided that since Trixie was a mut, she was not good enough to be with his prized canines.

So he decided to take her into town, a long distance from where we lived and turn her loose into the ritzy part of town where she would find a really good home.

He put her in the trunk of his car so she could not see where she was going and he also took the long way round over the hill country. Then he came back by way of the short-cut. That way he could be sure she would never find her way back. He did everything as he had planned, but my husband was not prepared for what happened as a result.

He returned, and had no more than walked in when there was a scratching at the door. He opened it and I thought he was going to faint! There stood Trixie! When he could finally catch his breath, he said, "Come on in old girl. You can stay!" She did and remained my kid's Guardian Angel Dog all their growing up years!

CHAPTER SEVEN

My Ghost Dog

I must tell you about my "Ghost Dog." As a child, every night there was a big black Doberman pinscher with eyes of fire that stood beside my bed. I wondered all my young life why he was there. I felt sure he was not real flesh and blood, for Mother would never allow a dog in the house.

I had to keep him a secret. I had seen Angels and fairies as a child and I floated on clouds but when I tried to tell my family or friends they ridiculed me or accused me of lying. So I had to keep the knowledge of my "Ghost Dog" to myself. Though he was there big as life every night, he remained my very own secret.

I was a little afraid of him, though there was no reason except he was so big and his eyes looked like fire. I had never heard anyone speak of Angels much less in the form of a dog. I really wanted to know why he was there. I thought it might be because I was a sickly child and he was there to protect and comfort me.

One night I decided that I just had to know; was he an Angel or was he a real dog? It took a long time for me to muster up enough courage to stick my hand out from under the covers and try to touch him. After many tries I finally did it. My hand went right through him! I tried it again and again and each time, same thing.

So now at least, I knew he was a spirit; a ghost ... but why was he there??? I found out after my daughter was married and was living in another state.

Alice called and told me of her horrendous experience. She was driving her convertible with the top down, when she suddenly came upon an underpass from which a big truck was emerging at a rapid pace and she was about to plow right into it. The truck was so big she would have run under it and she would have been beheaded. She said, "Mom, I swear a huge black dog, a Doberman pinscher with eyes of fire, jumped up on the hood of my car, causing me to slam on the brakes. That dog saved my life! But can you believe this? As suddenly as he appeared, he vanished into thin air!"

For the first time, I told her about my ghost dog. Now I know why he was there at my bedside each night. He was an Angel in animal form to protect not only me but those I love. He was my Guardian Angel. So you see, Angels can take any form they desire at the time they need it ... human or animal! Since I was a little kid and could probably accept a dog easier than an Angel, my guardian took on that form.

CHAPTER EIGHT

Gene and Bubba

Here is a different version of how a deceased loved one, who is now an Angel, can affect an animal who has loved her dearly. I met my friend Gene, whose wife had passed on soon after I had lost my dear husband. I walked over and spoke to him and his dog, Bubba. We found that we had a lot in common.

We became good friends. I visited him and his dog, Bubba but the atmosphere in his house was just dreadful. One could feel the grief that still hung heavy in his entire house. After a couple of visits, I suggested that he allow me to lead him in a "spiritual house cleaning." I told him how we could clear out all the grief.

His dog, Bubba loved Gene's wife. He had been her dog. Bubba would not go near anything that she had used or a chair she had sat in, nor would he go near the bed she slept in.

As Gene related all this to me, I knew that house must have a through cleansing. So we lit a candle and sent a cleansing Christ light through ahead of us. Gene carried the candle. We went through the entire house, room by room. We visualized the Christ Light going ahead of us sweeping through each room as we went, cleaning away all the dark, heavy energy. We then clearly saw the beautiful Christ light flooding every room and filling it with love, peace and joy as Gene dedicated each room and himself to God.

As we made the full circle back to the living room, it felt like we had just pushed the walls back and the light and love flooded the whole house. It was miraculous! To this day the house feels much larger.

But what surprised us both, suddenly I almost shouted, "Gene, your wife is here!"

Her presence was so obvious, even Bubba knew it. He went over and laid in what was her favorite chair, which he would not go near before. He now loves everything that had been her personal things and lays on her bed. The house is so full of love. Her presence fills each room. She could be the Angel who brought Gene and me together for this very purpose.

So if you have never seen an Angel nor felt the presence of a deceased loved one, maybe it is because you know they are invisible which makes it hard to believe. But if you will just be open to their presence, they will appear whether visible or invisible.

If you could speed up your vibrations or the deceased one could slow down theirs, you could see them. We have grown to believe that this physical body is what we are.

Not so; this physical body is just the house we live in and it doesn't even belong to us. God only loaned it to us for a short while. Remember He speaks of our body as "His Temple." The spirit which lives inside of this body is the "Real You."

"Most all important things are invisible." Think of it! You cannot see God, but you know He exists. That knowledge is instilled in all of us. You can't see the wind, but you can see its effects. You can't see laughter, but you can hear its melodious tones. You can't see love, compassion, joy, caring, thoughts, pleasure or grief, but you know they all exist.

Einstein said, "The real world is invisible. If you can experience it through the senses, then it is not the real world."

In other words if you can see, hear, taste, touch, or feel it, then it is not of the real world. Why ... because the beta brain waves govern your senses and compose only 5% of your mind.

It helped immensely knowing that several of my psychic friends as well as my daughter could see Lou in my house even if I couldn't. I felt his presence so clearly I believe because so many others did see him. I had no problem at all understanding what he wished to relay to me, as you will see as I reveal some of the miracles he brought about very soon after he passed on.

At such times, we need all the help we can get. I thought, being a counselor all these years, I understood another's problem, but I found that I really did not know how much another was suffering until I actually experienced it myself. I am endeavoring to help those who have suffered grief and disillusionment through death of a loved one. I pray my book helps.

One person I counseled for years and helped through her husband's death was so disappointed in me when she saw me fall apart at my husband's death; she told me she thought I was above such things. She seemed to forget that I also inhabit a human body, with human emotions and feelings.

I doubt that anyone can help very much with the first shock and loneliness of losing a loved one through death. But I can teach others some things that helped me recover and get back to where I could be a whole person again. The shock helps for a short time. You are so confused and do not want to face what is happening. Shock is like a buffer for a short time.

We must allow the grieving process according to our own individual pace. Just know that grief is natural and self-correcting. The grieving process enables us to recover from a very devastating wound. With the proper perspective, you will eventually see that it is God's instrument for healing a broken heart. We find that grief itself is a medicine.

Crying is therapeutic and helps release the heaviness. Grief, like many negative, unpleasant situations over which we have no control, must be allowed to run its course, to come to the surface in order to be released.

CHAPTER NINE

Advice to the Grieving

There is no way to release anything until it surfaces. One lady told me that she couldn't release her grief for several years. When she finally sat down and re-lived the death of her husband and brought it to the surface, she was able to cry and let it go. Then she was able to pick up the pieces of her life and begin to live. Lou came through to me and told me to go upstairs and sit down on our bed and re-live that horrible experience and cry as hard as I needed to. I knew he wanted to help me so I agreed.

I thought I would never make it up those stairs and re-live that awful night when his precious lifeless body fell onto the floor beside our bed. Oh, how that hurt, but re-living that awful grief and crying so hard helped me release more grief which I really needed to do. I found that every time I let go and just cried and sometimes pounded a pillow, even screamed, it helped to release more pain.

This is also how our planet gets ready for ascension ... by releasing the negativity through tsunamis, tornados, earthquakes, and hurricanes. Mother Earth must lighten herself to rise into the fifth dimension with us aboard.

The grieving process has been likened to a journey across a stormy lake. The death of a loved one launches us into a tempest of emotions. We are surrounded by darkness and heavy waves of despair. Comforting words are drowned out by howling winds of sorrow. Our only companions are loneliness and horror, our navigators, ushering us toward a new stage of life, which we do not understand.

The days immediately following this tremendous loss are filled with numbness, unreality, anger at the one who has gone on, and anger at God for taking him or her. One point I would like to make: when we are so angry and hurt at God, the one who has gone on and ourselves, one thing is certain. When I cried and screamed at God, telling Him that I hated Him, He just loved me all the more. I could hear Him saying, "You are just proving how much you know I am in charge and that 'I Am All There Is.'"

As the actual fact that the loved one is gone sets in, absolute horror takes over and we sink into depression. We ask, "What is there to get up for? Why even try? My reason for everything I ever did is gone!"

Finally we arrive at the time when we must begin to try to see a light at the end of the tunnel. It is so hard, but we must try for our loved ones and friends who have stood beside us. We can affect the deceased loved one's growth and ascension if we hold on too long. We can't do it for ourselves at first, but it helps as those who have suffered grief tell us that it will get better. I found that as I began to realize that it is not all about me, and began to put my attention on others, I began to realize that we owe it to the world to reach out to them.

As we do this, we find that the world responds; slowly at first, but I found that it really does get better. Your loved ones and friends do not know whether to come and try to comfort you or whether to leave you alone for a period.

Then we must learn to love ourselves. Even though you don't want to, make yourself a good breakfast; go shopping; buy something that brightens up your environment.

Each time I go to Wal-Mart, I treat myself to a blouse. Wow, do I have a large selection of blouses! My daughter laughs as she calls me and asks, "Did you treat yourself to a new blouse this week?"

Call friends, talk to God and yes, talk to that loved one who has gone. Yes, talk to that Angel. Most everyone who has been down this path told me it might take a year or sometimes two to even get to where you want to be part of this world again. I found that was true for me. Oh, I still have a good cry when something sparks a fond memory, but that is good therapy. I cry often as I write this book.

In my counseling, I hoped I had helped those who were grief-stricken but I hadn't a clue as to how much they were suffering until it happened to me. We don't really understand anything until we actually experience it ourselves, which is why I am endeavoring to help those who have suffered grief and disillusionment through death of a loved one.

I doubt that anyone can help much with the first shock and loneliness, but I can teach others some things that helped me recover and get back to where I could be a whole person again. We must allow the grieving process according to our own individual pace. Just know that grief is natural and self-correcting. The grieving process enables us to recover from a very devastating wound. With the proper perspective, you will eventually see that it is God's instrument for healing a broken heart. We find that grief itself is a medicine.

I also found a good way to release grief is to use the "Scream Therapy." Being a counselor, teacher and writer I often taught this kind of therapy with great results. Take a pillow and scream into it as loud as you can. Scream at the grief, the feeling of anger, of how you hate being abandoned; pound that pillow as you scream! No one will hear you, and you will find that the feeling of being silly will vanish as you experience the release. This tremendous therapy empties out the hurt, the desperation, the loneliness and feelings of injustice you are experiencing. If you will give this therapy a try, you will find yourself going back to it every time you feel this overwhelming emotion setting in. As I used these techniques and began to try to help myself, I began to feel my husband's presence.

For instance, I learned that it was hard for my husband to get through to me while I was in deep grief. When my daughter came and stayed with me, offering companionship and love, and my dear friends offered their comfort and understanding, as I could pull out of some of the extreme grief, it was then that my husband could get through to me. It was when he told me that he is now my guardian angel. If Lou had not told me, I would have known it is true because of the many miracles that have transpired since his death.

A man who is psychic, and had never heard of me or my husband, told my daughter who lives in another state that her mother's deceased husband is now her guardian angel and that he always will be. He said that if I have a problem or need guidance, all I need to do is to become very quiet and tune into my Guardian Angel Lou and he will be there for me. I have done so many times since my husband died and found he is always there for me.

I want to share many miracles and incidents that Lou and I experienced together while he was still alive as well as the ones since his death.

CHAPTER TEN

Premonitions of Lou's Death

As I look back, I can see there were quite a few premonitions of Lou's impending death. I tried not to see them or talk about them. I could not face ever losing Lou. As an example, we were returning from a book signing and seminar which I had conducted in Cape Coral, Florida and, as we rounded a winding curve in the road, I looked up. To my amazement, there was the most perfect profile of Lou. It was not part of a cloud but clearly painted against a white cloud. I exclaimed, "Oh, honey, if only you could take your eyes off the road for one minute, you would be so amazed at what you would see. Your profile is huge and stands against a white cloud!"

But Lou could not take the chance and by the time we were out of that winding curve, it was too late. I remember asking him what he thought it might mean, but I didn't pursue it because I was afraid of what it might reveal. Lou died about nine months from that time.

There were many different incidents when I had feelings that I did not understand. It was all part of that uncharacteristic fear or insecurity that I could not put my finger on. It was a knowing that I did not want to accept, like the same fear concerning that awful black hole which I experienced before Lou died that I could not explain. I experienced it again after my husband's death.

I felt as though I had been completely deserted. I could not pull myself out of that awful blackness. I experienced that black hole that Job of the Bible went through; not once but twice ... once before he died and again afterward.

I could never face the fact that some day Lou might die before me, even though he was a good bit older than me. I couldn't let myself think about that. It was far too painful to contemplate. But I found that all of this was a preview of what I experienced when he died.

I think Lou consciously or unconsciously knew he was on his way out. Just a day or so before Lou died, I suggested that we get into the Jacuzzi which we did on a regular basis. Lou said, "You go ahead and let me just sit here in my lounge chair."

I replied, "Honey, I don't want to be in the Jacuzzi without you. It wouldn't feel right."

But he insisted and I finally did, but I felt really alone.

Another probable preview concerned our tall Grandfather Clock which Lou loved. He loved the chimes and he always wound the clock.

On this particular night I was ready for bed and Lou was well settled into his lounge chair, so he asked me to go ahead upstairs and let him stay put. He slept there all night.

When I came downstairs the next morning, I found one of the huge weights that control the chimes on the Grandfather clock, lying on the floor. I immediately picked it up and put it back in place. I said, "I didn't know it was possible for those huge weights to fall."

Lou replied, "It didn't fall. I took it off the hook. The chimes were bothering me."

That made no sense at all. Lou loved everything about that clock, especially the chimes. Since then I have wondered if this may have been a means of him trying to stop time. Did he know that time for him was running out?

And many times when I had my hands on his body I said, "If you were not here in the physical, I would know you are here in spirit but oh, how I would miss not being able to touch this precious body, this house you live in!"

Was I feeling an insecurity that there would be a time when I would not be able to touch him?

I remember Lou and I many times talked about ascension and hoping that Jesus was coming soon. We planned to be ready, together to go with Him.

I said to Lou, "I just heard that our ascension is just around the corner, some say probably within months. We could stand on our heads that long. Couldn't we, Honey?"

He answered, "You bet we could!" So why was I feeling some insecurity about us being together when we ascend, why that particular conversation and the following one?"

I must have had a knowing that something awful was about to happen. I am very intuitive and I sense things. But if that was it, I'm just as sure I could never have faced losing Lou. That was too painful to even contemplate, which was probably why I went into shock when he passed on. I could not accept, that like Job of the Bible, "The thing I feared had come upon me."

It seemed that if one of us had to go first, I would have been the one. But actually I do not believe that Lou could have survived my death. Even though Lou was quite a bit older than me, I was the one who was always in jeopardy because of things like spine surgery, e-coli, heart attack, stroke, shingles, etc. Lou was always so tender and caring, no matter what. Every time I was in the hospital, he slept downstairs on the couch. He could never go upstairs to our bed until I came home. He was always there to take care of me with such love. Here is a poem I wrote to him during one of my many challenges. I placed a copy of it in the Casket with him. I called it: Loving Sacrifice

Darling, I could never doubt your love
You've been a wondrous companion to me
Have put my health above your own
Been as strong as I need you to be
I've never known a bigger man
I've seen you work straight through
Finishing a task that I began
While asking nothing for you
You've loved and cared for me tenderly
When it looked like all was in vain
Not once complaining, always sustaining
Though it hurt you to see me in pain
Without a doubt, you've loved me more
Than I could ever be worthy of
Your caring, sharing and patience
Surely have proved your love

To my precious husband
(Chosen for "Sounds of Poetry," Outstanding poets of 1994)

CHAPTER ELEVEN

The Hologram Miracle

Both before and since Lou's death, we had many miraculous happenings that cannot be logically explained, like the hologram of Jesus that graces the mantle of our fireplace. It came about very mysteriously.

We were at Countryside Mall. Lou was occupying his time just walking around the mall while I took my organ lesson. He was obviously excited as he rushed over to me, "Honey, you must come with me. I just know you are going to want a miraculous item I just found!"

He knew that I loved anything concerning Jesus. We hurried to the little store where he had found a most astounding Hologram.

I couldn't believe what I was seeing! Jesus just came alive!

He returned every move I made. If I bowed to Him, he bowed to me. If I turned my head, he turned His head in the same direction.

When I reached out my hand, Jesus reached out His hand.

"Of course I want it. This is absolutely unbelievable! I didn't know anything like this existed!" I exclaimed.

So Lou bought it and we brought it home. It was almost midnight and they were closing the mall as we left. We could hardly wait to get the Hologram into our own living room on our very own mantle! We put up lights to show it off. What a miracle!

I exclaimed, "The first thing in the morning we must go back to the mall and tell that store manager to order a big supply of these Holograms. All my friends and acquaintances are going to want one. Remember they said we purchased the last one."

So we were there when the mall opened. We hurried back to the spot where we had purchased my Hologram. There was no store—only a blank wall! We couldn't speak for a few minutes ... we just stood there staring at each other. How can this be? We went to the store to the right of that wall and asked, "Where is that store which was here last evening?"

The business owner looked at us as if we were out of our mind and answered, "What! There has never been a business there."

I went to the store to the left of where that store stood the night before. "Where is that store that was right here last night?" I asked as I pointed to the blank wall.

I got the same surprised look as she replied, "I don't know what you are talking about. There has never been a business there."

We were more confused than ever. We went back home and we looked that Hologram over from stem to stern and found only one phone number. I wasted no time in calling it.

A very sophisticated voice answered, "There is no such number." I tried several times and each time I got the same response.

I thought, "If there is no such phone number, how can you be answering it?"

We have shared this Hologram with almost everyone who visits us and there have been many. Everyone has been blessed in some special way. Everyone is overwhelmed as Jesus responds to their every move. It is amazing. As you bow to Him, He bows to you. When you close your eyes, he closes His. If you bend or reach out a hand, He does the same. Jesus just comes alive!

Many miracles have resulted from people just giving their problem to Him. I tell everyone that if they need help or have a problem, to just give it to Jesus. I explain to each one how to maneuver until Jesus puts out His hands—then just give those problems over to the Master.

I remind each one that once he or she hands it to Jesus, it is no longer their problem—anything from financial, marital, health, whatever the problem—it is taken care of.

One man was healed from cancer in his eye. He was here recently to thank Jesus again for his healing. I can think of two occasions where a person needed surgery but each was too weak to be put under anesthesia.

Both of these men had been in the hospital but found they were too weak to be anesthetized. As their wives each called me for counsel, I told them to bring their loved one and have them give the problem to Jesus. They both did and each one was able to have the much needed surgery.

Many people have been healed. Some came to ask Jesus' help in business situations; some had money problems. Whatever the situation it is never too big for Jesus!

I'll share with you a typical example. God told me that the young man who was doing some work for me had a big problem. So I went to him and asked, "Young man, do you have a problem?"

He answered, "Oh God, yes but how did you know?"

I took him to the Hologram and turned on the lights. I told him to maneuver until Jesus reached out both of His hands.

"Now take every problem you have into your hands and just give them over to Jesus."

I left him alone with the Hologram. A while later, he came into my office, tears streaming down his face and exclaimed, "When I came in here, I was so burdened I wanted to die; now I do not have a care in the world!"

This is typical of what happens almost every time we share the Hologram. This Hologram has become a big part of many people's lives as well as our own.

CHAPTER TWELVE

Ashtar and the Ball of Fire

Another big influence in our life has been a huge red ball of light that fills our bedroom doorway every night since we moved into my big house. It has been there every night and is still there since my husband's death.

When it first appeared and for a long time afterward, we tried to find out why it was there and what was its purpose for being in our doorway. We would often go over and stand in the doorway with the light surrounding us and we felt so comforted and at peace.

I called many famous and some not so famous psychics to see if they could tell me what that huge ball of light meant. Most everyone felt it was a symbol of who or whatever was there to protect us. Finally one very psychic lady who came to visit exclaimed, "Do you mean to tell me you don't know that huge ball of fire is Ashtar?"

I was surprised and delighted! Ashtar has been very close to me for several years since I had a channeling by the famous Michael El-Legion. He channels Sananda, Ashtar and Archangel Michael. The entire hour is recorded on tape and I listen to it often.

It came about as a result of my meeting Michael El-Legion. A friend called and asked me to accompany her to where Michael was making an appearance. After the speech, I got up to leave and I heard a voice over the crowd. I looked around and Michael was beckoning to me. I asked, "Me?"

"Yes. Will you please come over here?" He asked.

I walked over to where Michael was sitting. He said, "You need to sign up for a session with Ashtar. He has many things to tell you."

Then he explained that he channels Ashtar, Sananda and Archangel Michael. He insisted that Ashtar was telling him that he had much to reveal to me. I tried to put him off. I really didn't want to pay what I considered a big fee for a channeling. Finally Michael, said, "This is so important. I will greatly reduce the price and even come to your house to do the channeling. It is that important! Ashtar knows what he is doing!"

He explained that the session would be recorded and I would receive a copy of the tape. So he came to my house and did the taping. That tape has become one of my most precious possessions.

I listen to it often. The information is timeless. I should explain that at the time of the channeling, Michael leaves his physical body and one of the entities takes over Michael's voice box. I actually talked to Ashtar and asked him questions.

He told me that he has been with me for a very long time and especially when I am writing. I know that he even now stands at my shoulder along with my other Spirit Guides when I sit down to write. And I do feel his presence as I am writing, even now.

It was shortly after this that a red ball of light appeared in the bedroom doorway. Ashtar has become a very real part of my life. He has revealed many truths to me.

He was the one who gave me a preview of the black hole I was doomed to encounter. I talked to Ashtar about this black hole. He explained it was much like what Job of the Bible went through. I experienced this less than a year before Lou's death. It was the same as I experienced when he died.

Ashtar also told me Lou and I would ascend into Heaven which we did while Lou was alive. He said our ascension in that other dimension would be for two-and-a-half weeks which we found is equivalent to five hours earth time. I'm so thankful we had this fantastic experience together before Lou died. I tell about this experience at length in another part of the book and explain how time is different up there.

Thank God, Ashtar is still with me every night … as that ever-present red ball of light.

I want to make this completely clear: this and all the miraculous feats I relate to you in this book were not anything like a dream. We were wide awake the whole time, more alive than we had ever been in our entire lives, not only while up there but for many hours after we returned. As a matter of fact, after our ascension, I don't think my feet touched the floor for three days!

PRELUDE TO OUR ASCENSION

Ashtar recorded on the tape that Lou and I would ascend into Heaven, but I still cannot figure why a letter would trigger such a feat—that is, if it did!

It was 3 AM, the very hour when I nearly always awaken to go to the bathroom. I began to read a letter from Jim Carter, the owner and discoverer of the Miraculous Twilight Products. I read through the first couple of lines of this letter and began to feel extremely light and absolutely euphoric!

I am very familiar with this feeling, for it is the beginning of what I experienced when I died and went to Heaven! Wow, what a thrill! Once you have experienced the euphoria of ascension, the memory never dims.

I had been telling my husband for some time about Ashtar's prophecy that he and I were going to ascend into Heaven while still here on earth, just like when I died. The only thing that I questioned later was that the prophecy said our ascent would be for a period of two-and-a-half weeks.

We were gone a little more than five hours. We timed it! More about this later on in the book.

I had no problem believing what Ashtar conveyed to me for he had told me so many things and it always happened. But what did concern me was that Ashtar plainly said we would be gone two-and-a-half weeks.

We were gone a little more than five hours. But after much research, I found five hours earth time is equivalent to two-and-a-half weeks in that other dimension.

Up to this time Lou was really afraid of dying. I could never get him into my astral projection class. He said he did not want to get out of his physical body. But after being in Heaven, he was no longer afraid. After being in his spiritual body, he never again feared death. Up to this time, Lou—like so many—believed his physical body was who he was. He found that the real Lou is spirit, not physical body.

Lou, like so many others, chose to leave earth at this time for a very special reason which I explain earlier in the book. He gave up his life for my daughter's. He felt because of his age, she could be here for me much longer than he could.

Death is such a frightful thought for those who have never been out of this physical body. Many choose to take the short way home.

This is the reason for many incidents which most of us consider tragic ... not for the one who goes, but for those who love them and are left behind.

CHAPTER THIRTEEN

Why So Many Are Leaving Earth

Most people know we are at the end of a cycle that ends with earth's ascension and are frightened. Many do not want to be here when the earth, along with all who are still on Planet Earth, go into that fifth dimension. Many made this decision before they incarnated on earth the last time.

This is why enlightened ones study and work so hard to make sure they are ready. When we raise our consciousness, it not only expands our DNA function but also increases our vibrations, a process of getting earthlings ready for ascension. So, we look forward to that delightful experience! We realize that this is something wonderful to look forward to. But many would rather not know about such things.

These dear ones are choosing to leave Planet Earth before the ascension takes place, and they have the right to do so. Most everyone knows we are near the end time that signals Jesus' return.

He told us that we would ascend along with Him the same as he returned to Heaven the last time ... in His physical body.

We are going to go with Him in our physical body. A friend and I had a preview of what it is like to ascend in our physical body. You will read about it in this book. I called it "Seize the Moment."

Ascension is so near and yet many, actually millions, are choosing to leave before it happens. There has to be something very big to accommodate passage for these many dear souls. They must have a means of entering into Heaven.

This is why the tsunamis, earthquakes, hurricanes, tornados and flooding must take place. These people need a route whereby to leave. They either consciously or subconsciously chose one or the other before they were born. These dear souls cannot just go out there and commit suicide! This is a means also for Mother Earth to lessen her burden and become lighter which she requires for her ascension.

And even though we grieve to think of so many in what seems like horrible deaths, there really is no pain associated with death. I know, for I have been there. Death is absolutely a blessed release ... so beautiful. One could never imagine the freedom, the beauty, the euphoria of being in Heaven until it is experienced.

I read about a family who saw the tsunami coming and knew they could not outrun it. They joined hands and sang the "Alleluias" as they were swept into Heaven together ... a blessed release for them.

Our hearts go out to the loved ones left behind. These dear ones are not grieving for the ones who have gone, but rather for the tremendous loss of those they love as they must go on without them.

You will read of several incidents dealing with this in this book. Pray for the dear ones who are left behind. They hurt. I know, for I've been there.

CHAPTER FOURTEEN

Death Is Like Astral Projection

Death is much like bi-location or astral projection (where one leaves the physical body and goes into the spiritual body), except death is much more euphoric. I teach Astral Projection in several different colleges and it is taught in many of our very fine universities.

We are actually talking about feats that even today are considered impossible by some. If you have never had the blessed experience of leaving the physical body and going in spirit to other places and then returning to the physical body, I can understand that it could be fearful.

Bi-location is almost the same, the difference being that in bi-location the person can actually be seen in two places at the same time. There are not many recorded cases of bi-location.

In astral projection the person is not seen in bodily form by others. One travels in the etheric (the spirit body).

I have experienced bi-location quite a few times, though I am aware of being in only one place while others see me somewhere else. Bi-location is rare. It has not been experienced by many people, though the Bible does give a few accounts. The following reveals several examples of my own bi-locations.

My daughter has seen me in her kitchen many times, though she lives in Ohio and I am in Florida. I asked her if it was like seeing a ghost. At the time I only am aware of being in Florida.

"Oh, no, it is nothing like that; you look as real as when I am actually with you. It is wonderful. You never talk to me. You just walk around and watch me as I prepare the meal," she said.

I took a leave of absence for six weeks from Yoga class because I needed to be at the College for that period. The Yoga instructor had a rare experience in my absence.

She insisted that I was at our Church during Yoga Class every Thursday night, as always. I said, "Martha, you know I am at the College every Thursday night. How clearly do you see me?"

"Exactly as I see you now, and don't think I am nuts. There are five of the students who see you every Thursday night, doing Yoga right along with the rest of us. Furthermore, I called the College and they confirmed that you were there at the same time."

Another bi-location experience happened not long ago. It was revealed to me as I went for my usual walk down at the pier. A young man who works at Wal-Mart asked me why I walked right past him without speaking that very morning.

I assured him that I had not left my house until late afternoon to go to the pier. He said, "You were wearing the same outfit and same sandals that you are wearing right now ... even your painted toe nails were the same."

I asked him if he knew about bi-location or out-of-body experiences. He answered that, yes, he was aware of this. He had studies in such phenomenon and understood.

Two famous cases of bi-location come to mind that are recorded history.

One involved Milarepa, a Tibetan mystic. He was seen by his followers in his physical body in Asia, India, Ceylon and the Malay States at the very hour of his death.

The other one was Monsignor Alphonsus, the Abbot of Arienzo in Italy. This was authenticated by the Dominican Observatory and Augustinian Orders. While he was in a deep sleep at the Monastery, he was also in Rome leading prayer for the dying Pope.

So, since we all acknowledge that things are not always what they seem, why is it so difficult to believe that almost anything is possible?

Einstein said, "If man can think of it, he can do it!" Scientists will confirm that we leave our bodies each night during sleep. If we did not let the body rest in this manner, we would not live very long. That our loved ones, who have gone on, are in a different form which is invisible to us only means that their vibrations are speeded up, but that does not mean we have no contact with them.

Please, if you are grieving over a deceased loved one, tune into him or her and listen to what he is trying so hard to get across to you! Listen for that very first message. Remember, as I said before, it will be that very first thought—not the second or third!

By the time the second thought has come through, you are into your beta brain wave frequency. This will not help you. Your beta brain wave only accounts for 5% of your mind.

It takes the other 95% to reach one who is in that very high vibration—Heaven! And it will be the very first thought! I repeat, when dozing or when you are into the very first stages of sleep is the best time to get in touch with that deceased loved one. Remember that you alternate between the alpha and theta brain wave frequencies as you sleep ... that 75% to 95% brain wave frequency.

Many times when we awaken and begin to remember a dream—it seems so real. That is because most often it *is* real ... not a dream.

CHAPTER FIFTEEN

Mine and Lou's Ascension into Heaven

The experience I am about to relate to you happened while my husband Lou was still here on earth with me and I was wheelchair bound. It was nothing like a dream. We were more wide awake than we had ever been in our life during the entire journey. I reiterate, Ashtar had told me that Lou and I would ascend into another dimension while here on Planet Earth.

I really was not that surprised when it happened. I got up at about 3 AM and went to the bathroom. I picked up a letter which had come in the daily mail and began to read. I almost immediately began to feel so-o-o-o ecstatic! Lou entered the bathroom about that time and I handed the letter to him. He read the first few lines and exclaimed, "Oh, what on earth is happening to me? I am feeling something very strange and wonderful!"

I fairly shouted as I took hold of the railing, "Hurry back to bed. Remember I have been telling you we are going to ascend?"

Grabbing my arm as we scampered back to bed, Lou exclaimed, "You promised to hold my hand!"

Remembering that Ashtar said we would be gone two-and-a-half weeks, I said, "Let's look at the clock. We must know how long we have been in that other dimension."

It was 3 AM. We became lighter and lighter and were moving very fast when Lou shouted, "My body is as light as a feather. Wow! Is this how it feels when a person leaves his body?"

"Exactly ... I have tried many times to tell you what it is like, but it is impossible to describe!" I answered.

"I'll say. There is no way a person could explain this! I never in my wildest dreams thought I'd get to experience anything like this!" Lou answered.

To make a five-hour-long story short, this was just like the experience I had when I died. We were taken to the same place. The euphoria is so magnificent, there are no words to describe it. But as we scurried about Heaven, I said to Lou, "Isn't it just great that I got to show you what it is like to go to Heaven and even show you where I went when I died?"

We were flying. I say flying. I didn't see any wings, but we were moving very fast and our feet were not touching anything. We were praising God from tremendous depths we did not know existed.

There is no way to imagine the absolute serenity and peace and yet such exhilaration. We laughed and cried for sheer joy! The light coming from God was so bright we could not see Him, but we knew it was God. It filled the heavens! One would think a light so bright would be blinding or would have hurt our eyes, but it did not. Lou asked me, "Do you think God might let us stay here in Heaven?"

I reluctantly answered, "Probably not. When I was here before and I knew He was going to send me back, I begged, I argued, I cried, I tried to bargain with Him. He just kept telling me I had work to do back on Earth."

So He sent us back. But Lou and I had manifested our dream of being together when it came our time to die, we thought. We had made a pact that neither one of us would leave the earth without the other. We had experienced our vision, our proof, for we had lived our dream. God gave us a preview. No doubt about it; we reveled in the assurance that we would indeed get to go to Heaven together when it came our time to leave this earth!

In our minds, God had just proved it to us. Ashtar had told me that we would ascend, but he said we would be gone two-and-a-half weeks. As I relate in another part of this book, we found that two-and-a-half weeks in that dimension is equivalent to five hours earth time.

I think this explains why I went into absolute shock when nine months later God took Lou back to Heaven to stay, and left me behind. That was what the preview was all about! The preview was for Lou to have a glimpse of where he would be going nine short months from then.

I shouted, "Hey, wait a minute, didn't You forget someone?"

Back to the story: as we returned to earth, we looked at the clock and it was a little past 8 AM. We had been gone a little more than five hours! But the exhilaration stayed with us for days.

CHAPTER SIXTEEN

I Was Doomed and Then Healed

I must explain why this is such a profound story! Before this trip into heaven, I had been doomed to a wheel chair for the rest of my agonizing life. That is where I was when we ascended into heaven...doomed to a wheelchair!

What put me in a wheelchair? Here is the story: Spine surgery seemed the only answer. The surgeon had to cut a piece of bone from my hip to cover the huge hole that resulted from the surgery. There are large screws holding it in place. My spine continued rapidly deteriorating. I had been in a wheelchair for two years and finally all my doctors and my surgeon, even our family doctor had to give up on me. They all gave me the same diagnosis. They had done all they could do.

They all told me I would have to learn to live with that awful pain and remain in a wheelchair for the rest of my life! I would never be able to stand more than three minutes at a time. I was devastated. Everything in me is shouting, "No, no, no!"

"That was the stage of my life when we ascended into heaven! Here is the picture as we returned from that five-hour ascension that will just astound you as it did my Family Doctor when we went for our regular annual check-up a few weeks later. I still couldn't see why Lou wasn't healed as I was during our five-hour trip into Heaven.

Now remember my doctor had seen me just a few weeks before this visit and gave me her diagnosis along with my surgeon and my other doctors—that of being doomed to a wheelchair for life.

I walked into my Doctor's office and she almost fell off her chair, as she exclaimed, "Where is your wheelchair? And how can you be walking and looking and acting like a kid?"

I calmly answered, "I'd say I am healed, wouldn't you?"

"But, you can't be. I just don't understand! What in heaven's name could bring about such results?" She exclaimed, all in one breath.

I told her all about our five-hour trip into Heaven. She did not argue when I told her I was off of all my medications.

I did not see her again until a year later after Lou's death. I went for my annual checkup. Being the wonderful physician she is; she just held me in her arms and cried with me.

I thank God that I got to show Lou where he would be going, and the way. But at the time of our adventure together, little did I know that our wonderful ascension before was a preview of the real thing. That was nine months earlier. His death followed our format of ascension exactly!

It was the roughest time of my life, but what a "victory" for him! As much as it still hurts, I am happy for Lou's good fortune. I wouldn't call him back if I could.

My very psychic friend, Glenn, called and told me that he saw Lou as he ascended into heaven. Glenn told me how he saw Lou sitting on the side of the bed when he began to rise higher and higher as though there was no ceiling, and on into heaven.

His description was exactly the way Lou and I had ascended together nine months earlier.

Glenn said, "As Lou rose up toward the ceiling, he looked back and saw his body sitting on the side of the bed. Lou chuckled and exclaimed, 'Well, for Heaven sake, and just kept going."

Glenn did not know that I had brought a urinal into the bedroom suggesting that Lou use it. He had bumped his leg on a concrete step while bringing in the groceries. Since we were planning another cruise right away for his birthday, which would be in two weeks, and another trip to Hawaii in April, it seemed best if he stay off that leg for a while. He was treated at a nearby clinic, given tetanus shots and anti-biotics, then released.

The 911 crew who came when I called attested to Glenn's description. They said Lou had been sitting on the side of the bed using the urinal when he passed over and his body fell across my legs. They couldn't believe what they were witnessing: no sign of struggle nor shortness of breath. It was as if he did not die; he just left the body.

I have thought since and I hope all of you reading this will give this some thought—think of how awful it would have been if we had gone to sleep angry at each other without our usual good night kiss and the words, "I love you."

Let me give you my prospective of what happened. It was around 4 AM. I felt Lou fall across my body. I awakened with a shock and said, "Darling, what are you doing at the foot of the bed?

"Here," I said, as I reached down and took hold of his arm, "I'll pull you up." But he slipped off the bed onto the floor.

"Oh, my God," I shouted as I ran around to the side of the bed realizing that something was dreadfully wrong! I called 911 immediately. By the time I got downstairs they were at the door. Lou had already made his ascension when his body fell across my legs. The 911 crew affirmed this.

CHAPTER SEVENTEEN

Lou Gave His Life So My Daughter Could Live

I know now that Lou made an agreement with God to give up his life in exchange for my daughter, Alice's, because he felt that if she could be healed of that awful heart condition, she would always be there for me. Since he was a good bit older than me and she was still young, she would be around much longer than he would.

Just before all this, Lou and I had gone to a "Benny Hinn Healing Crusade" for ourselves and we stood in for others who couldn't be there, like my daughter, Alice.

I vividly remember, while at the Benny Hinn Healing Crusade just as Benny stepped upon the stage, Lou excused himself to go to the bathroom. It seemed a bad time to leave the scene since Benny was just beginning his healing service.

Lou was gone so long I became really concerned. When he finally returned, he was in a real state of confusion and he looked like he had been through some horrible ordeal. He didn't tell me anything except that he had gotten lost in that huge auditorium. That made no sense as he has always been a great navigator no matter where we were. It was just not like him to get lost!

I believe that wherever he went during that time, Lou was making a bargain with God. He believed so much in my work. He had explained many times that he believed helping me was the real meaning and reason for him being on Planet Earth.

Though we went to the crusade for ourselves, we also stood in for others who could not be there. My daughter was one of the ones I stood in for. So we left with no visible signs of healing.

All that evening and on the way home Lou was preoccupied ... even to the point of having symptoms of not being well. A nursing home attendant was on the same tour bus with us. He stayed close to Lou and checked him often. But he felt sure that Lou was not having a heart attack.

I was very much concerned after we returned home. Lou began having spells of vomiting, loose bowel movements and shortness of breath. I begged him to let me make an appointment for him to either go to the hospital or our doctor and have a thorough check-up, but he would not agree to either, and when I insisted, he would become very upset. Several times I felt that I had to call 911, but this upset him even more and each time I had to back down.

My daughter, Alice, had a very weak heart and was not expected to live but a short while, which is why I stood in for her at the healing crusade. She was getting steadily worse.

After we returned, Alice called me and began to explain how some kind of a force knocked her to the floor twice. As she was explaining what happened, it sounded exactly the way it happens in Benny Hinn's healing crusades.

People just fall under the power. Benny will raise his hand and at times the entire congregation will just fall flat. Kathryn Kuhlman, during her lifetime did her healing crusades the same way with the same results. Alice had been told that she could die any time, so when she fell to the floor, she thought, "This is it."

After some time and she realized she was still alive, she decided to see if she could make it to the bathroom. She made it and was very surprised. She reasoned, "If this was another heart attack, how come I can get up and I don't have that usual horrible pain in my chest. This was the way she and her doctor expected she would die. Normally after one of these attacks, her chest would be so sore she could not touch it.

My daughter had not seen the Benny Hinn Healing Crusades on TV so she did not understand what was happening. So as she was telling me all this, I explained that this is exactly the way people are healed in the Benny Hinn healing sessions. I told her I had stood in for her when I was there.

From this time on, Alice kept getting stronger and Lou kept getting weaker. This continued until Lou's death, soon after this.

Right after Lou died, Alice called and asked me if I wanted her to fly down here to be with me. I told her, "Of course not."

I knew she could not even step outside in her former condition. She was so weak she could not even get in a car. But she insisted that she would fly to Florida to be with me.

Fly down here from Ohio??? In her former condition she could not get on a plane if her life depended on it. She insisted on coming.

Lou had only met my daughter once. So after his death when she came to comfort me, I thought it strange that Lou appeared to her thirteen different times, yet I have not seen him since he passed on.

She was so changed. While she was here, she painted almost all my downstairs walls and ceilings, completely redecorated my whole house and worked so hard. We shopped for sixteen pair of new curtains—and hung them, a complete make-over of my entire house.

This was when I realized why Lou was in such a dither at the Benny Hinn Healing Crusade. He was bargaining with God to let him give up his life for Alice's.

He now communicates through Alice. Through him Alice knows any time I need something or when there needs to be a change in my life. She has become my confidant, my advisor and guardian. Through him she knows everything about me and my needs.

I feel a very strong presence and I communicate with Lou telepathically. She saw him plainly. I have a Hologram of Jesus on my mantle. He just kept coming to Alice through the hologram.

Since my husband's death, Alice gets clear messages about anything that might affect me in any way. She will be told when to get someone out of my life. This happened several times. She is guided as to when I should take a certain action, and she lets me know when I am in harm's way. This continues to this day. She knows it all comes through my husband who is in Heaven.

I feel a tremendous responsibility to do whatever God put me here to do. Lou believed so much in my mission, he gave his life so I could finish it. He loved helping me as I wrote my books and articles. Many miracles have come about through him since his death. He is still helping me.

This book actually began as a section of another book, but when my publisher read the synopsis, he said, "This is too good to be just a section of a book. I think it needs to be a book in itself. I can see it helping many people who have gone through the grief and trauma that you have just experienced."

CHAPTER EIGHTEEN

Our Last Cruise Together

I must tell you about our last cruise together. Our 79th cruise was aboard "The Carnival Sensation." On each of our cruises God has worked through us to bless someone in a special way. Most often it is a healing, or God had a message for someone and used me to get His point across. God allows His healing to come through me and I never know what form it might take.

Lou and I were a team. God always told Lou who needed something. He would then point them out to me. It never failed. God would then work through me to counsel them or to do a healing. Having been a counselor and healer for years, my training always came in handy.

In almost all instances, long before I realized someone needed help, Lou would point out a person in a wheelchair or just someone needing help. I would wander over to where the person was and would seemingly bump into them just so I could put my hands on them. I usually tried not to let them know this was a healing touch.

I have found that it is good practice when doing a healing, that the person who is being healed be unaware of it. That way, their negative faith cannot get in and affect the result.

What? You don't know about "Negative faith???" It works! Why is it so powerful? Because 95% can doubt something, but how many positive believers do you find?

I call this "healing in absentia." Negative faith works against a healing just as positive faith works to insure it. Note this is why I insisted that my husband not tell his son where his healing came from in the following article about healing Charlie's feet.

CHARLIE'S FEET HEALED

At the time this happened I had never heard of healing in absentia. I had never met my husband's grown son nor had I ever heard of this type of healing. We were on our way home from a dance as Lou began to tell me about how his son suffered so terribly from very thick calluses that caused horrible pain to his feet. He could hardly walk. His son needed to have surgery, but he would be laid up for some time and he could not afford to lose his salary.

As I listened to my husband tell of Charlie's disability, suddenly I exclaimed, "Darling, if I had Charlie's feet in my hands right now, I could heal them" (meaning God through me). As I said this, I suddenly felt as if I really had Charlie's feet in my hands. I began to go through the motions of rubbing away those awful calluses from Charlie's feet.

I was exclaiming how awful this condition was. I rubbed his toes, soles and every area of Charlie's invisible feet one at a time. I kept up this motion until we got home.

I said to Lou, "When we go inside, I want you to sit at the end of the couch. I am going to lie down at the other end and place my feet in your lap. I want you to massage my feet."

I continued, "As you are massaging my feet, I am going to transfer the soothing feeling to Charlie's feet. I want you to visualize along with me, Charlie's feet receiving this healing, loving touch." This continued until we went upstairs to bed.

The phone rang very early the next morning. It was Charlie. He practically shouted, "Dad, you're not going to believe this but my feet are perfect. I do not have a pain. I haven't been to a doctor nor had any treatment—absolutely nothing, yet my feet look and feel wonderful. Can you believe this, Dad? I have brand new feet! I don't know how this can be, but I swear it is so!"

Lou covered the phone with his hand and whispered, asking me if he could tell Charlie why his feet were healed. I motioned and whispered to Lou, "No, No!"

Lou whispered again, "Please, let me tell him!"

I shook my head motioning, "No, no!"

After he hung up the phone he asked, "WHY wouldn't you let me tell Charlie where his healing came from?"

"We can't be sure that Charlie could accept such an unusual healing. If he should doubt it, he could reverse his healing. We don't dare ever tell him."

To this day Charlie has no idea why his feet never hurt any more.

We are all part of universal intelligence and the wisdom that runs through divine mind is ours for the asking. This universal intelligence manifests in many different ways.

It can be in healing, psychic gifts, counseling, channeling, the arts like painting, sculpture or any creative endeavor.

We are all channels through which this power can flow. Some of us may be better channels, perhaps because of our awareness that it is possible, or it could be because of incidents in our lives, which have made believers of us.

I find that often when we encounter persons who doubt the power of this tremendous energy, it is because that person has never had an experience from what we call the "Supernatural." I feel blessed that I have been chosen to be a channel of this energy.

Healing is one vein that I have manifested through, but often I am not sure of the route the healing might take. The power may come through my hands, my eyes, or through a phone call. I must relate another very special time when God chose me as His instrument:

FRANK'S EYES HEALED

My husband and I paid a visit to our friends, Paul and Tony. We did not know they had company until they left the room and returned, leading a gentleman, one on either side of him. They introduced their friend and explained that Frank was blind. They seated him in a chair next to the couch where my husband and I were seated. Almost immediately Frank reached out to me and took hold of my arm, holding on tightly with both hands.

He explained, "I don't know why, but I feel a power coming through you so strong I can't turn loose of it. I can't see your husband, but I hope he will understand. I have never felt such energy. It is like electricity. I can't remember feeling such a force in my body since I was a child."

Notice that Frank was the one to recognize this power and where it was coming from before I did. I had no idea that I was to be the channel through which this healing energy would flow to Frank. Why does a certain person know when this power is available? Frank was very surprised but also very receptive to this power.

As an example, how did the Centurion know that Jesus could heal his servant even from a distance? Remember, he told

Jesus that he was not worthy to have Him enter his house, but he knew that, if Jesus would just say the word, his servant would be healed. Somehow, the Centurion knew.

And how did the woman who had an issue of blood know that Jesus would heal her? Jesus was probably not aware that she was even in the crowd. But somehow she knew that if she could but touch the hem of Jesus' garment, she would be healed. Remember, Jesus said to her, "Thy faith has made thee whole."

I whispered to Frank, "Don't worry. Lou understands. I just want you to direct all this healing energy into your eyes."

The four of us continued our conversation as Frank held firmly onto me. Every few minutes he would exclaim, "I have not felt so alive since I was a child."

Each time he made such an exclamation I would turn to him and repeat, "You are experiencing God's healing power. Just keep directing the power into your eyes."

This continued for about an hour or more and then we left. Neither Paul nor Tony said a word about Frank's outbursts. Later that evening we had a call from our friends. "You won't believe what happened this afternoon! We took Frank out to dinner and can you believe this?—he read the menu!"

A few weeks later, Frank got his driver's license. If there is anything great in any of us, it is the creative force expressing through us. The Divine Mind's nature is to create. Most great artists admit that there is an unseen creative principle which works through them to accomplish their feats of genius. God's healing energy works the same. So, you see why it is so easy for me to believe this tremendous potential. There is no limit to it!

We have always known that in blessing others we also bless ourselves. And it also improves our consciousness. When we help someone else, it not only expands our DNA but also raises our vibrations for the process of getting earthlings ready for Ascension.

Our words and thoughts, when sent out with intent, go out into the earth consciousness (the ethers) and form a grid which is accessible to everyone. And as we do this, everyone around us will feel it. Just know that any words or thoughts (good or bad), when sent out deliberately, will give the effect intended.

Each time we experience a miracle or visualize a healing, it goes out and affects at least 100,000 people. Just think of that! I often think of this when I am doing my morning meditation, knowing that I am affecting 100,000 dear ones for good! So beware of what you allow into your mind at all times, especially before going to sleep and when near water! Water is very receptive to your thoughts.

So as we planned our seventy-ninth cruise (not knowing it would be our last together), I suggested that we set up a "Love Grid" around our ship which would make this a spectacular cruise for everyone aboard.

"How can we do that? I can see how we can do it for ourselves, but for everyone on board? What do you have in mind?" Lou asks.

"We will set a 'Love Grid' over and around the entire ship. Most people think only Angels can do such things. God put everything under man's dominion, and then he made the Angels to help us. We so often under-evaluate ourselves. If we knew how really powerful we are, it would scare us to death."

"Okay, Sweetheart, how are we going to do it? This one is beyond me," Lou said.

"We become very quiet and get in touch with our God mind. While in this meditative state, we will visualize a beautiful golden cloud of God's love engulfing the entire ship with all the people, even the workers, so very happy and loving with everyone on board."

We continued our visualization each day 'til we set off on the cruise. As we boarded the ship, we could already feel the love grid working. This was our seventy-ninth cruise and we were anticipating it to be one of our best.

It turned out to be our most memorable, just four short months before Lou passed on. The cruise was to celebrate his birthday which would have been the 17th of September. He died September 4th. I am so happy we had that last beautiful cruise. The night he died, we were planning our eightieth cruise and our next trip to Hawaii. We had made a practice of going to Hawaii every two years and this trip was almost due.

Back to the cruise ... it was easy to see the love grid was really working. People were feeling it; we could tell. They seemed to even know somehow we had something to do with it. No matter where we appeared on the ship, people reached out to us and wanted to talk to us and share experiences and just be with us.

The maitre d' left his post long enough to seat us at a special table for two and was very generous with the phrase, "I love you."

I decided to really test the love grid. If you have been on many cruises, you know one does not question the rugged Band Director on deck about anything, especially about being too loud. So I went over to the Band Director and plainly told him that his music was too loud. He looked at me and asked, "What are you saying?"

I repeated, "Notice when you start up your band how everyone on deck seems to steel themselves against the loud music. Then tone it down and observe how they seem to blend right in with it."

This big tough Band Director took my advice and then said to me, "You know, you were right. I would never have believed that before. Thanks for your suggestion."

My husband couldn't believe what he was seeing. As I returned to my lounge, he stated, "Well, it is obvious the love grid is intact and working miracles. That is wondrously obvious!"

So it continued throughout the entire cruise. Of all our seventy-nine cruises, this was our most memorable.

For a long time following Lou's death, I could not even think of that cruise or the other wondrous events that made up our life.

All I could do when I thought of them was regret Lou's demise and cry my heart out. Even now as I share this with you, I have crying spells. As I try to help others who are suffering, I find peace in showing them a brighter side.

Just think, since that loved one has gone ahead of us into heaven, we now have our very own Guardian Angel. If you ever doubted the existence of Angels, you have no need to ever again.

Most of us know that the body which we cherish is not the person. It is a temporary dwelling. This body doesn't even belong to us. God only loaned it to us for a short while. I repeat, "God refers to our body as HIS TEMPLE."

CHAPTER NINETEEN

Other Miracles

MY BUSINESS CARDS ANOINTED

My last Easter Spent with Lou was phenomenal. It began when I accompanied a friend to a little Shrine where she had known many miracles to have happened. We lit a candle and, as we put in a donation, we each picked up a tiny plastic zip-locked bag which contained a small cotton ball which had been soaked in anointing oil. I dropped mine into a special place in my purse and forgot it for a time.

Later on Easter morning in what we refer to as our "Angel Room" upstairs, as we were getting into meditation, my angel reminded me of the cotton ball. I just knew the angel was telling me that Lou and I should anoint each other with it. As I reached for my purse, I remembered that I had dropped the anointed balls of cotton into a special section of my purse where I keep only my business cards.

As I reached into that special section of my purse, my hands were suddenly dripping with anointing oil. I was astounded because that cotton ball was in a very small sealed plastic bag and it was dry. I placed it on the table. I reached back into that section and was shocked! Every one of my business cards was dripping with oil. But the real surprise came as I noticed that somehow I had placed two of someone else's ordinary business cards (not laminated as were my own) in with my cards, and they were dry as a bone.

I grabbed a paper towel and began to wipe the oil off my business cards on both sides and my hands which were dripping with oil. We looked at each other in utter shock as I placed the two other cards (completely dry) to the side.

Our next surprise came as I took another paper towel with the intention of trying to dry out that section of my purse. Wow! It was completely dry—no oil. It was absolutely dry! How could all the cards and my hands be covered with oil and that section of my purse be so dry?

Lou and I had seen many miracles, but this was different! We sat for a moment wondering what was the meaning of all this. Now I wonder if it was all because this would be my last Easter with Lou?

We weren't prepared for what happened as we finished our service. I walked over to the mirror to apply some make-up and found my face and my glasses covered with gold dust. We remembered that not long before this, we had seen gold dust pour down on Benny Hinn's head and shoulders, and then on another occasion the same thing happened in Paul Crouch's religious service. I learned a long time ago not to try to explain miracles. I just accept it and am thankful.

I WALKED ON WATER

I want to share another miracle with you. It was when I walked on water. I believe that everything Jesus spoke is true. He said that the things He did we can do and he added, "Even greater than these shall you do."

This reminded me when Jesus walked on water. Peter was so thrilled that he got out of the boat and began to walk on the water toward Jesus. As long as he kept his eyes on Jesus, he was all right, but the minute he took his eyes off Him, he began to sink and Jesus had to rescue him. Yes, I walked on water.

Lou and I went to Howard Park where we could swim in the surf. This part of the gulf is very large and dolphins come in close sometimes and swim with the people. I have always loved dolphins, and as a group of us were out where the water was very deep, a pod of dolphins swam close by. I was so excited! I shouted to the other swimmers, "Hey, look at these beautiful dolphins" as I began to count them. I counted out loud up to nine dolphins as I pointed out each one when someone asked, "What are you standing on?"

I stopped counting and answered, "Come to think of it, nothing." So she said, "If you can do that, so can I" as she pushed me aside and took my place. Plunk! Down she went. Another swimmer came over and tried it. —Plunk, same thing! They all took turns pushing me aside and trying, but each with the same result. It got to be a game. Those on shore began swimming out to where we were, and each one tried it with the same result. They began asking my husband what I was doing. He laughingly answered, "Oh, she thinks she is Jesus Christ. She thinks she can walk on water!"

They answered, "She is doing a pretty good job of it." Then they began to ask me if I belonged to that Greek Church where so many world famous miracles had occurred ... the statue of the Madonna actually cried etc. They told us of how there were many wheelchairs, crutches and canes outside the church as evidence. As I said before, I don't try to explain these miracles, but I believe in my sharing them with you. If you have not experienced miracles, perhaps you will begin to realize that, if it can happen to me, it can do the same for you.

CHAPTER TWENTY

Vibrations and Telepathy

That precious one you adored is now an Angel—a spirit just as he has always been. We have all at some time in our life allowed ourselves to believe that our body is the "real me." When our loved one has left the body and we can no longer touch it, we realize how precious this "God's Temple" really is. God has taken it back.

Our deceased loved one is still with us. We just cannot touch him or her. I appreciate so very much being able to tune into my husband's spirit. This is how we communicate via telepathy.

You might think it unfair that a psychic can see your dear one and you can't. The reason I want you to understand this is, once you begin to grieve (which we do every time we think of him or her), our vibrations are thrown back into a 5% ratio.

I was able to receive Lou's messages via telepathy. In another part of this book I go into detail and explain that the reason you cannot see the one who has passed on, though you can feel their presence and even communicate via telepathy, is that their vibrations are much higher than when he or she was in human form.

A psychic person can actually see a deceased person when they go into a trance state; their vibrations speed up. When their vibration is equal to the deceased person's vibration, they actually see that person just as he or she was before death.

Of course in your mind's eye you can see them. You do this every time you think about them. You cannot think without seeing a picture. Think of your loved one right now. Can't you see him or her—actually see how they smile or laugh or see that funny little quirk that is so familiar to you? Your loved one is very much alive.

You have seen him or her, touched him, lived with him and loved him or her. The body never did belong to them. I repeat, "It was just a house God loaned them for a short time."

So we must realize the same applies to our own body temple. It is also only on loan. It doesn't belong to us. As for our loved one who has moved on, God has taken that temple back. He will do the same for us some day, unless the Ascension happens before that time.

In that case we will ascend in our physical body just as Jesus did right before His disciples. They watched as He ascended in His physical body straight into heaven. A moment earlier He was telling them that just as He ascended (in His physical body), so would they ascend in the last days. And is there anyone who doesn't believe we are living in the end time?

Either way, when a person leaves this earth, he or she is at home with God. But that loved one is more alive than ever. It is just that he or she is in spirit form.

If we leave this earth before Ascension, we will go in spirit, but if we leave along with Ascension, we will take our physical body with us. Jesus told the disciples that we will be changed in the twinkling of an eye. Our physical body will be made perfect as we ascend ... just think, "In the twinkling of an eye!"

To see something or someone in the spirit world you must possess the same rate of vibration as it or them. This is why we do not physically see our deceased loved ones, because when we think of them, we drop down into that little beta 5% vibration because of the grief... nothing magic here. It takes a vibration of 75% to 95% to see Angels or those who have gone on.

You are more likely to see your Angels or loved ones who have passed over when you are awakening, or beginning to doze off. Why? Because at these times you automatically go into your alpha and theta brain wave frequency, which means your vibrations are much higher.

I have not seen my late husband, although I feel his presence and I hear him telepathically talking to me. When on occasion, we do see Angels, spirit beings or deceased loved ones, there has had to be a change in vibrations.

Others have seen Lou here in my house. My friend, Joanne, was sitting on the couch visiting with me when suddenly she seemed to be in deep thought, almost as if she had dozed off. She had drifted into a trance-like state. She said, "Lou was buried in a blue suit with a vest and turtle-neck shirt."

"How could you know that?" I asked.

She answered, "He is standing right here in your living room."

The higher vibration into which Joanne entered had to be the same as Lou's, which is what made him visible to her.

The most important things are invisible. You cannot see God, but you know He exists. That knowledge is instilled in you. You can't see the wind, but you can see its effects. You can't see laughter, but you can hear its melodious tones. You can't see love, compassion, joy, caring, thoughts, pleasure or grief, but you know they all exist.

Einstein said, "The real world is invisible. If you can experience it through the senses, then it is not the real world." In other words if you can see, hear, taste, touch, or feel it, then it is not of the real world.

I know there are those who do not believe that a loved one can become an Angel, but even if Lou had not told me that he is now my Guardian Angel, I would have known because of the many miracles involving him since he expired.

Though eventually we need to try to release the one who has gone on, I believe it is important also to tune into that one, from time to time. I find it helpful to talk out loud to my husband. At first, it hurt too much, but now I can keep a picture of him on my desk and even talk to him. I find it helpful also to include him in my morning meditation and prayer.

For instance if I plan to work on my book, I ask Lou to please come and stand at my left shoulder. That way when I feel his presence, I know he is helping me as he did while he was on earth. I know he is with me as I am writing this book.

During our life together, Lou and I found that the more we talked about the Angels here in our house, the more they made appearances. Sometimes we only felt their presence, but many times we have actually seen them. Lou often talked about the two Angels that were at my bedside at night as I slept. He saw them vividly, bending over me as if attending to me each night.

Our deceased loved ones have just stepped out of their bodies, and I am so thankful that death is never painful. Not only do I know this from my own experience, but ascended Masters such as St. Germain, the Archangels and Kirael affirm it.

KIRAEL TELLS OF THE SPACE SHUTTLE THAT CRASHED

A great analogy to what it is like to disengage the body and step into Heaven was described by the ascended entity Kirael, when he described what he saw from Heaven as the shuttle crew did just that, when the space vehicle, "The Columbia" exploded.

Kirael tells how he and the Heavenly Host watched from Heaven as seven dear ones were whisked into the loving light of the Creator. And as the human world suffered this tremendous loss, the Heavenly Host felt what the seven spirits felt as the space vehicle entered the outer realms of the planet.

He tells how all seven on board experienced great concern. Each had a knowing that something out of the norm existed. It was as if their higher selves began to transform the very particles of their life force.

He explains that no fear permeated the crew as the panels of the projectile began to give way in the extreme heat that held the craft captive.

He says that in these definitive moments, in what seemed like a heartbeat, all seven crew members immediately withdrew from the constraints of their physical human body and returned to the truth of their spirit body to access their chances of survival.

Kirael explains how they dislodged themselves from the shuttle craft and how they knew beyond doubt that they had been freed from this human world.

He said, "They stood united over a place we call the United States and emerged into an enormous light which was surrounded by the Angel Force. They drew the attention of all light, and for the briefest of moments humanity was merged to its natural state.

"From there," He said, "they watched as the space shuttle plummeted to earth with the remains of their human bodies. Their last and deepest desire was that all humanity would feel the force of united love."

MY FRIEND SHARES THE EVENT OF HER HUSBAND LOU'S DEATH

A dear friend shared her experience with me and gave me the privilege of sharing it with you. Her husband's name was also Lou. He was angry because cancer had caused his death. She said it took several months after his death for him to be brought into the light. When he finally emerged into the light, he came to her in what seemed like a dream with two of his brothers who had gone on before him. Of course she knows that this was so much more than a dream ... it was a revelation! We do have experiences that, although we are asleep, are real astral happenings.

She said, "He was so handsome, looking just like he had looked when we first met, and we each knew we were meant to spend our life together. I fell in love all over again."

She asked him to take her to the place he had occupied in Heaven and he did as she asked. She said, "No one could ever convince me there is no Heaven, for that was exactly where he took me. It was so beautiful, it is impossible to imagine what it looked like. The grass and the trees were the most beautiful shade of green, and the sky was so lovely, I can't begin to describe it. I am so blessed to have seen it. I still miss him, but I know when he is near.

He smoked a pipe when he was here on earth. At these special times I will smell the aroma of his special tobacco. Although I am married now, I will never release that part of him that was part of me. We were soul mates and always will be. The pleasures he shares with me are far greater than the pain of his death."

I say to all who are grieving, "Try not to cry too long, for it stunts our loved one's soul growth."

She suggested that since I have the opportunity to visit with Lou, I should, for it will speed up the healing process. She offers her precious help to me in any way possible.

She tells me how much my books have meant to her and how she has grown as a result of reading them. Friends like this are invaluable.

LENA HESITANTLY EXPERIENCES HAL'S RETURN

Long before my husband passed on, another of my friends lost her husband and was devastated. I said to her, "Maybe he will come to you in spirit."

She protested, "Oh, no, that would scare me to death! Besides, I don't believe in these impossible things I hear others talk about."

But about three months later, she just had to tell me of her very rewarding experience. She said, "I sensed that someone was in the room; you know how you feel a presence? I opened my eyes and there stood my husband! He didn't look anything like he had just before he died. He was the good looking, youthful Hal I married. Oh, he was so handsome. And it was not scary. It was the most wonderful experience of my life. Thanks for making me believe."

WILLIAM BLAKE'S DEATH

William Blake, the great poet and artist, spoke calmly of his approaching transition and looked forward to its occurrence. A friend recounted that his death-bed songs were "A Prelude to The Hymns of Saints … and overtures to the Choir of Heaven." It was a chant for the response of Angels. Then his spirit departed like the sighing of a gentle breeze.

My precious husband I'm sure can relate to that. Those who came to attend him after his death said there was no sign of struggle or even shortness of breath. It was as if he didn't die, he just left.

For those who find it hard to accept that Heaven, Angels, spirits and miracles exist, let me tell you, I have been to Heaven three times. I am giving you a few examples of others who have had that privilege.

JESSEE DUPLANTIS' ASCENSION

Lou and I loved watching the tape of the TV Minister, Jesse DuPlantis' Heavenly visit. He was very much alive, as you will see as he tells his magnificent experience. He was there almost the same amount of time as my husband and I. It was a little more than five hours. One must be in the spirit body (the real you) in order to enter Heaven, but it is not anything like a dream. Lou and I were more alive than we have ever been in our entire life, and so was Jesse.

Many dear ones ask how you will know when you are in the spirit body. You will know all right! You feel light as a feather. There is no weight to your body. You move about as though you are flying. You may or may not see wings, but you will call it flying, for as you move about, you realize your feet are not touching anything.

You might wonder why people who have had that privilege do not always see Heaven the same. That is because the Heaven you will experience, whether when you die or if you should have a supernatural experience, will be whatever you expect it to be.

As Lou and I ascended, I really hoped I would get to show him where I went when I died. And that is where we went. I got to take Lou right there and show him where he would be going nine months from that time. I'm so thankful I didn't have that knowledge at the time. Thank God, He did not let me know that this was a preview of where Lou would be going to stay in nine short months.

Having been to Heaven three times and having achieved the feat of astral projection and bi-location, I can tell you that it is all very exciting. But going into Heaven is far greater than astral projection, for you are truly out of this world. With astral projection and bi-location, you remain in the earth realm.

What is Astral Projection? This is the process or ability to leave the earthly body, emerge into your spirit body, and go to other places. I can tell you, getting out of this prison we call our body is a wonderful and exciting experience. Once you leave this physical body, you will never again fear death.

As you enter the spirit body and find yourself above, looking down at your earthly body, you will be reluctant to come back into the physical vehicle. Actually it is difficult to live on Earth once you have experienced Heaven.

I am including a lot of real psychic experiences for this purpose: everyone needs to know that this physical part of our life is not it!

If you can open your mind to accept the larger picture, this physical experience will be much richer and life will have so much more meaning. You will find that you are spirit, not body.

Astral projection happens often involuntarily, as in many recorded incidents of an automobile accident where a person tells of looking down and watching the rescue squad as they remove his or her body from the wreckage. Or often it happens during surgery. Most everyone has read where a person tells of looking down, at his very own body, as a surgeon performs surgery on it. There is never any pain associated with leaving the body whether in dying or temporarily.

This happens all the time. I recall many incidents that Lou and I experienced which many would think of as absolute magic. The following was one of them, where Lou and an Angel brought me back to life.

CHAPTER TWENTY-ONE

Flirting with Death

(published in *Fate* magazine)

Even though my husband was a great deal older than me, I never dreamed that Lou would die before me. I was the one who was always ill, injured, incapacitated.

A few years ago, when I was quite ill with a serious virus complicated by a heart condition, a strange thing occurred.

Although my doctor insisted I needed to be in the hospital, I refused to go. I knew my condition was serious, but I felt that if it was my time to go, I would die no matter where I happened to be.

On this very night soon afterward I stopped breathing. My husband Louis, who watched over me constantly, awakened with a start, sensing that something was wrong. He put his hand on my chest and realized that I was not breathing.

Something (he learned later an Angel) told him to turn me over and massage my spine. As he was telling me this, he was confused as to why he didn't just jump up and call 911.

He said that with each movement of his hands he distinctly heard a sound like the tone of a tuning fork. He said that the sound was coming from a few inches above my body. Each movement of his hands produced this sound, and it stopped only when I began to breathe. He then knew it was an Angel directing him and working through his hands.

Usually I am wide awake at the slightest touch, but I was unconscious or dead. I knew nothing of it. As all this was going on, I (in my spirit body) got up to go to the bathroom.

Obviously I could not have been in my physical body, or I would have felt all the commotion as Lou and the Angel were trying to get me back to breathing.

During all this commotion I was in the hallway where I saw a man and he openly flirted with me. He was leaning against the wall with his foot drawn up behind him. He was dressed in a completely black cowboy outfit, which included boots and hat. From somewhere I heard voices accusing me of flirting with the handsome stranger. When I denied it, they insisted I was lying. I asked the man's name. These same voices said, "His name is Death, and you have been flirting with him."

As Lou was telling me what had happened, I suddenly remembered. I did not recall this episode until then. It seems the voices I heard were right; I really was flirting with Death. This complete story was published in *Fate* magazine.

THE RUSSIANS OPENLY REPORT MIRACLES

I would like to make a point here for those who have never had a psychic experience. I know that for you, it may be hard to believe some of these extraordinary events. The Russians are presently proving many of these feats scientifically.

They openly teach things our Government will not even talk about. For instance they are happy to splash it across the headlines that they have developed a camera which, when placed over the solar plexus, will take pictures of Angels residing inside of the body.

And another one that made the headlines was when a blind girl was able to focus and actually see through the tip of her forefinger. Soon the spiritual (invisible) will be commonplace.

Another one that made the headlines was when manna—yes, manna—rained from Heaven just as it did as recorded in the Bible which nurtured the Israelites as they crossed the desert.

It is not too unusual for stories about ghosts, spirits, entities, even haunted houses, to appear in their headlines.

My house was at one time haunted. Everyone in the neighborhood knew it but me. I didn't find out until after I had purchased my big, old twelve-room house. It didn't take very long for me to discover that the house was inhabited by earth-bound spirit people, the very ones who had originally built the house.

Ghosts are really people in spirit form who have died and remain earth-bound. Many times it is because they have never given any thought to God.

It can be because the person did not want to leave Planet Earth at that time. Quite often there is a sudden death, and the person doesn't know to go on into the light. Thank God I was able to lead these dear ones into the light, so my house is no longer haunted.

I wrote this experience, entitled "They Didn't Know They Were Dead," and it was published in *Diamond Fire* magazine.

CHAPTER TWENTY-TWO

Before He Died, We Cleared up the Bay

I must share with you some of the tremendous miracles Lou and I experienced before he died. I had heard of others who were clearing up rivers, lakes and ponds by pouring the Miraculous Prill Water into these water sources. After the miracles we had experienced from our ascension, and using the tremendous Twilight products, I could believe almost anything.

So when I felt that God was telling me that Lou and I were going to clear up a very large condemned, unattended portion of Tampa Bay, and the muddy, horrible ditch which poured into it, I was ready to obey.

Lou was a little reluctant at first, but he soon got into it full-swing along with me. We began each morning, to pour 2 gallons of Prill water, one into the ditch and one into the bay, that stinky awful, condemned area. As we would pour in the water, we would think of how it contained all the God qualities and said a prayer of thanksgiving to God for healing the water and the land.

This part of the bay area was not only condemned, but it was a terrible eye-sore to the community; no fish, no birds, no one was allowed to go near that very large part of the beach; it was unattended and fenced off. It was nothing but a murky, filthy, dirty unkempt parcel of land and water with warning signs saying to keep out of this condemned area.

The ditch that ran under the street and into the bay was even worse. That part of Tampa Bay was never cared for. It was grown up in weeds and the filthy, murky shoreline and water was a disgrace.

We had many curious observers at first, but after a few weeks, people seemed to go along with it. Improvement came much faster than we expected. We were pleasantly surprised that it could happen so fast. Within only a few weeks we began to see results.

First to appear were minnows in the ditch. We noticed that, as the minnows got larger, they would transfer themselves over into the bay and smaller ones would occupy the ditch.

Almost immediately the doves, green parakeets, many types of tropical birds, herons, ducks, fish and shell fish began appearing.

In a short time we noticed that the fish in the bay were much larger and at times the ditch was so full of minnows that you could not see the water any more.

One delight that began almost immediately I will never forget.

A huge white heron, his big wings outspread, flew toward us. I thought he was going to fly right into my face. He stopped short and landed in front of us as though to thank us for our effort.

He became a permanent fixture as each morning he would perch himself in a spectacular spot just in front of us. He built himself a nest which seemed to be his throne. He met us there every morning. We would greet him with, "Good morning, King-pin."

Another sight that I will always value was one morning when the ditch was full of baby catfish. They were so crowded and were swimming in unison like a performing orchestra. Their motion was orchestrated. Their colors of blue, white and little yellow feelers blended with the movement. It was so fantastic that if this scene had been in the sky, I would have sworn they were Angels.

One of the biggest miracles happened early on as one morning I started to pour my gallon of water into the ditch. As I looked down, I called to Lou, "Honey, do you have an instrument with a long handle in the van? I see something very unusual in the ditch."

Lou came over and with a long handled rake, he hooked onto the item and pulled it up. We could not believe our eyes. Here was a huge conch shell, the kind that one only finds at Key West. We brought it home and I washed it and let it dry. I have always loved big shells and I have collected some really huge spectacular ones, but none to compare with this one.

It graces the hearth of our fireplace. I know an Angel placed that big beauty in the ditch for us, a reward for our outstanding effort and belief in God's message, and for having the foresight to do what He told us to do. I have often thought, "What if I had doubted the message where I thought I heard God's voice? That part of our beautiful Bay would still be a disaster.

It was almost like when God spoke to Abraham and told him to go to a far country. Abraham said, "I think God is telling me to do this. I must do it rather than take a chance that he really is telling me to go to that far country." What did God do as a result? He made Abraham "Father of all."

As we continued our ritual, it wasn't long before the condemned signs were taken down, large fish came, and birds of every kind appeared in droves; and then seats were placed close to nearby trees. Residents seemed to love sitting there while the kids waded in the surf leading their dogs.

Soon boats were being launched, and dear ones driving down to the bay to wash their cars in the surf—what a sight! We kept up our ritual of pouring the Prill water into the bay and the ditch until Lou's sudden death—12 weeks later. This was another Victory for Lou before he went to Heaven. The Bay is now on its own and doing quite well.

I just found that they are expanding that part of the park and adding wider sidewalks, more seats and an extra shelter. I just know Lou is looking down from Heaven and applauding their effort. Tampa Bay is now a vision to behold!

I feel very sure that all this was planned by God to make Lou's ascension the great event it was and a very good example for others. His experience is a blueprint of what to expect when it comes one's time to go.

One point I'd like to make: every time we handled the Prill water, whether here at our home or at the park, we made it a practice to think of God, His great love and the joy of knowing Him. I still do this every morning as I prepare my water supply.

Water is receptive to whatever you are seeing in your mind, so whenever you are near water, be very respectful. Be careful of your thoughts. Make sure they reveal something beautiful, like LOVE. And remember, your body is 80 to 90% water.

I hope that what I have shared here will keep people from fearing death. I repeat, "There is no pain associated with death. Death is really a magnificent release; a tremendous adventure. I know; I've been there. The hard part is for the loved ones left behind who must go on in their absence. Our victory will be when our time comes to leave the planet and join those who have gone before. Until then, let's give life all we've got! Let's make it count!"

If you find it hard to believe miracles, let me say that if I had never experienced such things, I don't know if I could believe. But I have had such experiences all my life.

CHAPTER TWENTY-THREE

Mine and Gene's Miracle

Let me share an example of a friend who said, "If only I could experience one miracle, then I would believe."

I feel there is another reason Gene had this same happening that I am relating next. I told God years ago that if He was going to keep sending me these miracles, like He has done all my life, that I wanted a witness to every single one of them. He has complied with my request ever since.

I am thankful Gene was chosen for this role. Now he says, "Nothing can ever make me disbelieve that miracle and oh, how I would love to experience another!"

Read the following article and realize that maybe you just need a deep desire for a supernatural experience. I had been researching and writing about our ascension which I believe is very near ... and I believe we will ascend in our physical body, just as Jesus did when he returned to Heaven.

What makes this experience so different from the other incidents that I share in this book, such as when Lou and I ascended into Heaven for five hours is: Lou and I ascended in our spiritual bodies. The following is a preview of what it will be like when we ascend in our physical bodies.

This experience was completely different and occurred after my husband's death. I ascended in my physical body. I know now that God was giving me a preview of what it will be like when we ascend into the New Heaven and New Earth that Jesus talks about when he went back to Heaven the last time. He went in his physical body. He is telling us that man no longer needs the death experience. The following is one of the most fantastic magical experiences. Pay close attention, as it will spell out what you can expect very soon.

"SIEZE THE MOMENT"

A wave of absolute youth and euphoria swept over me! And it stayed, full bloom, as I walked the pier and around the amusement park. I felt brand new—not like a child, but rather like a radiant, young adult, without a care. I have not felt so full of life, ever, except when I died and went to heaven.

I was re-born, beaming with absolute radiance! I felt new life bursting forth in every atom, every cell and molecule of my body. I knew I was part of all there is! Happiness exuded from my being.

I was full of God! I felt so light—like a butterfly, a bird or a puff-ball on a summer breeze. It was much like my euphoric death experience except, this was happening to my physical body. This had nothing to do with dying—this was life at its fullest!

I had no feeling of any effort whatsoever. I walked further than I have ever walked in my entire life! My soul was celebrating the wonderment and the freedom I was feeling, the sheer joy of being alive. I have never felt so alive! Pure ecstasy filled my physical self. Nothing mattered but the moment. No past, no future, just the ever present NOW! I neither needed nor wanted anything—I had it all! I knew I was part of All There Is!

I wished with all my heart and soul that this experience could last forever. Was God giving me a glimpse of what awaits us? Words cannot begin to express the freedom I felt from head to toe. Is this what Jesus talked about when he said that we would ascend just as He had—with our physical body intact? I know now absolutely this is exactly the way it will happen!

I found later that Gene, my friend, had the very same morning experienced the same thing when he walked in the same area of the Amusement park. I prayed, "God, what is going on? Please just don't let it end!"

That seed within Gene and me lives and continues to grow. We can feel it inside us. We have compared notes and we each think much younger, act and look younger than we did previously. We have noticed that almost every time we talk, whether on the phone or in person, we find something to laugh about. Neither one of us had much to laugh about for a very long time.

He lost his wife just six months after I had lost my husband. If there was anyone in the world who needed a reason to even smile, it was us. We cannot ever be the same as we were before this experience! Now, I am wondering how I can bring back this heavenly adventure.

As I pondered the magnificence of it all, I remembered a psychic lady prophesized that I would find the "Fountain of Youth."

Is this it? What is the formula? Have I found the Pearl of Great Price? I pray, "Please, God, just let me recapture it and make it live, not only for myself but for others!"

I thought that Gene and I were the only ones who had experienced this wonderment, but as I became involved in my research, I found that there are other Light Workers who have had this "young again" experience. I have no doubt. It is a preview of what we can expect when we ascend in the physical body.

This experience has shown me that Ascension is closer than we realize. We are not going to die, but rather we are going to ascend while in our physical bodies, just like Jesus did. Remember, He told us in the scripture, speaking of the "End Times," that we would ascend just the same as He did. He went back in His physical body and He plainly tells us he will return exactly as He went.

I believe, as do so many great writers and spiritual people, that man no longer needs the death experience. Is anything too hard to believe?

Someone said, "If man can think about it, he can do it." Thought, which often results in bringing forth our intuitive energies, is the most powerful expression given to man.

I was talking to my Heavenly Father last night just prior to going to sleep. I told Him I really wanted to experience that tremendous youth encounter again.

Well, I did, but it was while I was asleep. As I awakened, I prayed to thank Him, but I added, "I really wanted it to happen in the physical body like it did before when I was wide awake."

Gene has to really be convinced before he will believe anything. But he, in no uncertain terms, was telling me how his body has not felt the same since we had that experience, but that it gets better all the time; and no matter how tired he or I get, that "seed" inside keeps growing. We have each had three more experiences of the rejuvenation process. One happened very recently.

I went to bed more dead than alive at 8 PM. I was so weak and tired that I did not care one way or the other. I was awakened between 10 and 11 PM. I had a surge of life like Gene and I experienced down at the Amusement park, a preview of "ascending while in the physical body."

I felt like a teenager ... not an ache or a pain. I was no longer tired. I stretched and felt so alive as if God had given me a shot in the arm, only better! It stayed with me all night and the next day. I did more work than I usually do in a month. I really felt ashamed as I said to my Heavenly Father, "I really do appreciate that heavenly physical experience, but I meant for it to happen during the daytime hours and I want to be able to bring it back, often." I have done so three times.

Seek and You Shall Find! I have really been searching for that youth-activation process. I want to find the ingredients necessary to bring it all back full blown any time I wish!

I really believe what Eric Klein says in his book, *The Crystal Stair,* that it is not necessary for this generation to experience death of the physical body. I along with many others feel that man no longer needs the death experience.

He says we will ascend just as Jesus did with our physical body intact along with Planet Earth, completely transformed—every atom, molecule and cell. Our age will be somewhere in our early twenties. That seems to be the optimum age and is the age Gene and I felt during our fabulous out-of-this-world encounter.

I have found pertinent information in an article by Wm. Samuel in his book, *The Child Within Us Lives,* and also in Eric Klein's book. Eric channels Sananda, Ashtar, Archangel Michael and St. Germain. Klein postulates that Sananda (Jesus) says over and over that we are not going to die.

After much research, I found that Gene and I are not the only ones who have had this experience ... many have done so. But it becomes very clear that God just gave us a preview of what it will feel like when we ascend in our body along with Jesus and the Planet. My research revealed that there are millions of people who believe that it will be in this lifetime. The only ones who are going to die are the ones that want to.

It is my belief that we are being prepared for the ascension. I have re-lived that experience several times since, but for only a short period of time. I can see that while on Planet Earth, one probably could not stay in that celestial bliss. It is so far beyond our earthly existence, we would not want to come back down to earth and complete what God brought us here to do.

Or as William Samuel in his book, *The Child Within Us Lives,* says, we need to come back to "earthly ground" for very good reasons and that is to try to share the mystical experiences we have encountered ... or in other words, what good would we do for the "rest of our self" if we just "lived on the mountain-top"?

In Samuel's book, he tells how he and others have been so blessed ... and I was delighted to find that the wonderment re-appears from time to time, as it does with Gene and me. I want to find how to bring it about more often and then teach it to others.

As I understand it, Samuel is saying that the Christ Child, which we are, is manifesting life with the innocence we lived as a child.

We had no hang-ups, fears, worries, aches or pains. It was enough to just be. I know that during this wonderful experience I needed nothing, I wanted nothing; I had it all!

This experience came about just as Venus began her momentous transit across the Sun, which was the most forceful about the middle of May and has continued through the end of June; and it does not end there but will continue until 2012. However we do not wait for 2012 but continue our Ascension process in the meantime.

This force is showering us and the planet with millions of particles of pure Light. This new energy is bringing us into the higher consciousness necessary for ascension. Our physical as well as our spiritual bodies are being prepared for ascension, and higher vibration is a necessity. Our Spiritual Hierarchy has been working on every atom, cell and molecule of our body for a very long time as we sleep.

The recent hurricanes, tornados, flooding, changes in the tectonic plates, and storms are examples of how Mother Earth is doing the same … getting ready for ascension.

Bad feelings, hurts and injuries—whether to Mother Earth or human beings—must come to the surface in order to be released so we and Earth can be light enough to Ascend.

Even our DNA is involved. We are definitely being prepared for ascension. A special period began July 16, 2004 and continued through August 28th, 2004, but it does not stop there; this was just a time to be especially mindful of the electric waves of light being sent into our cells, re-awakening our soul, thereby creating the appropriate qualities to facilitate our Ascension.

This is a time of light and loving energy, a reawakening of the soul/spirit strands of DNA. This soul/spirit DNA is located in the master DNA cell of the pineal gland. It is sending electrical waves of light into the other cells of our body during this special time and beyond. Pay attention! Be aware of what is happening!

Try never to think a fearful thought. Do you know that when you allow fear to enter your mind, your immune system shuts down for six hours? So beware! I don't want to even think of being defenseless for six hours ever!

I keep a good positive atmosphere in my home at all times. Everyone who comes into my house feels the Angel presence. Angels will not stay where there is negativity.

In another part of this book I tell about the Angel room and the Hologram of Jesus which I believe is one big reason I almost never come in contact with a negativity, here in my house or otherwise.

For instance, I had large crews of men working to restore my house after the five hurricanes we experienced during several different occasions. These men were from different companies, different professions and different trades, yet everyone who worked on my house was a spiritual person, believing in God and Jesus and, yes, Angels, even the contractor and the companies.

The men who cut down the huge trees which were struck by lightning were spiritual. At the same time, I also had to have the sewer line replaced from my house all the way to the street. These people and the company which they worked for were great believers and proud of it.

CHAPTER TWENTY-FOUR

The Angel Room

Two of the young workers had to pass through my "Angel Room" to get to the upstairs sun deck. As they came into the Angel room they sensed something which caused them to stop in their tracks and ask what they were feeling.

I asked them what it felt like. They said without hesitation, "It feels like Angel wings."

I explained that they were in the Angel room and that they were feeling the presence of Angels. I asked them to sit down at the table and become reverent for a moment. They were both overwhelmed. One of the young men exclaimed, "I have never felt so loved! I didn't know there was this much love in the world."

To make a long story short, they each asked if they could set up an "Angel Room" in their home. I assured them that of course they could. They asked me for recommendations. I told them that if they did not have a full room to devote to their Angel Room, they could use a corner of their bedroom or some other room where they could have privacy.

I suggested there should be a Bible or Holy Book on a table, one or more Angel statues and a candle, possibly some incense, and if they have a figurine or a picture of Jesus, to use it. I explained that they must keep a positive atmosphere at all times.

Angels will not tolerate negativity of any kind. This applies to anyone who enters their sacred space. The boys were surprised when I suggested that they bow their heads and invite the Angels to go home with them, stay with them and guide them. I explained that there are so many Angels that there is always enough to go around.

I tell this to almost everyone who enters my Angel room. This seems to overwhelm most people, that I would even think of parting with any of my Angels.

These young men both now have an Angel room in their home and are teaching their friends how to set up their own "Angel Room."

I explained that if a negative person did happen to enter that sacred space there is recompense. You do a thorough spiritual house cleaning. We need to do this every so often for our homes.

I teach people to do a spiritual house cleaning every so often. You begin with a rededication of yourself and your home to God. You visualize a Christ light sweeping each room clean. Go through each room with a lighted candle and visualize each room filled with spiritual healing power. Next you invite your Angels to occupy the entire home.

This reminds me of an incident when a lady whom I had counseled for a very long time called and told me that for years she had dreams of some day having a place on the beach. She said, "Now, I finally have my condo on the beach and it looks as lovely as I had dreamed it would, but it feels just awful in here. I can't stand it!"

I advised her to do a "Spiritual Cleansing" for it. I explained that when someone leaves a residue of negativity or a bad feeling in a previous habitation, whether home or business, the place must be cleansed from stem to stern.

I gave her instructions of how to do this just as I have explained above. She called me in about fifteen minutes. She was jubilant as she gave me the good news, "Oh, I am so happy! Now my place feels as wonderful as it looks. I love it! Thank you for informing me what to do!"

CHAPTER TWENTY-FIVE

Get Ready for Ascension

Now you might want to get into another type of Healing power to get ready for our ascension. There is a formula for activating the Youth and Vitality Chromosomes which will increase your vibration rate: It goes like this:

If you have a cyber-optic poster available, use it to get into your Theta brain wave frequency much faster.

You will find this fantastic poster in my book, *Metaphysical Techniques That Really Work.* But regardless, you must relax. Become very quiet within. Slow down your breathing. Feel yourself becoming almost limp. You are feeling very light, much like a feather in a breeze.

See in your mind's eye a very peaceful scene, like a bird gliding just above a quiet lake. Let it permeate your mind.

Feel yourself rising. Keep moving upward until you reach a distance of sixty-seven feet above your head, which, I am told, takes you above gravity.

One easy way to figure out the distance is to look at a tall two-story building and realize that 67 feet would be about twice that height. The higher you rise, the deeper you will be into the Theta brain wave consciousness. Any psychic venture requires you to enter your "Alpha or your Theta" brain wave frequency. Alpha is good but Theta is better. As you relax into Theta, use this prayer:

Father, Mother God,

"I command activation of the Youth and Vitality Chromosomes. Show me the Master Cell (remember it is located in the pineal gland in the center of your head—visualize it).

Now say, "Activate the remaining 44 Chromosomes, giving 10 new strands to all 46. Thank you. It is done! It is done! It is done!"

I can just hear someone saying, "Where do you get off commanding God?" I answer, "Remember you are part of God. God is the ALL THERE IS, but you are a part of the ALL."

Also the scripture says, "Command me now and I will open up the windows of Heaven and pour you out a blessing so big you cannot contain it." He loves us so much He made the Angels to serve us.

Use the information in this book and know that you are now ready to ascend, most probably in your physical body as did Jesus, and join your dear ones who have gone before. I don't think you will have long to wait. Ascension is upon us. By now I hope you have all experienced the magic of "Making Love with God!"

About the Author

Audrey Craft Davis is a published author, writer, lecturer, entrepreneur, and a veteran teacher and counselor. She has earned doctorate degrees in Divinity, Psychology and Metaphysics. She is included in *Who's Who of American Women* and *Who's Who in American Education* as well as the Register of Honors, *Dictionary of International Biography* of Cambridge, England.

Audrey is known for her work in radio and TV. You can find her other books and information listed at the end of this book along with where and how they can be purchased. Her books have kept her busy with book signings, seminars, workshops and classes. She also writes for several magazines.

Her books on practical metaphysics are featured in many other countries as far removed as The Luminous Wisdom Foundation, Ghana, West Africa and The Radiant Light Centre Library of Nigeria. Her book, *Metaphysical Techniques That Really Work* (Blue Dolphin, 2004), was featured at amazon.com for six weeks and rated five-star.

Audrey lives in Oldsmar, Florida and has a grown son and daughter. Her dear husband, Lou, passed away in 2002.

Metaphysical Techniques That Really Work

Audrey Craft Davis

ISBN: 1-57733-128-1, 148 pp., 5.5 x 8.5, paper, $14.95

Metaphysical Techniques That Really Work will guide you in the unfolding of your higher spiritual and mental potentials. Author Audrey Craft Davis describes the techniques and offers true stories from her personal experience. Next, she guides you with step-by-step instructions on how to use the technique and incorporate it into your life. With a little practice you'll learn to do the following:

- **Initiate contact** with your unseen guidance and earthbound spirits.
- **Bi-location**—projection techniques that allow your astral body to be seen in a different location.
- **Energy boosting** that will last for hours.
- **Numerology**—a short course in the magic of numbers and how to use them to your advantage.
- **The law of prosperity**—harvest the abundance that is your spiritual right.
- **Storing subtle energy** for later use with levitation, psychometry, healing and astral projection.
- **Do-it-yourself past-life regression**—a simple technique requiring no hypnosis.
- **Communicate with the spirits of departed loved ones**—several techniques.
- **Instant alpha trance** with a "Cyber-Optic" visual.
- **Aura reading**—the electromagnetic field can reveal more than you know.
- **Ultra-powerful healing techniques** that really work.
- **Much, much more!**

Metaphysical Encounters of a Fourth Kind

An Exacting Science

Audrey Craft Davis

ISBN: 978-1-57733-204-6, 144 pp.,
5.5 x 8.5, paper, $14.95

This book will teach you to apply Metaphysical principles to every area of your life, especially in achieving what you want. First you will learn Treasure-Mapping and Cyber-Optic viewing.

Your thoughts are totally powerful. If you think your world stinks, it does, but if you think it is lined with rainbows, it is. Change your thought; change your world.

Do you know that love is the greatest force in the world? Wrap yourself and your loved ones in the magic of love. Scripture speaks of it as "Putting on the whole armor of God."

- Learn to communicate with those on the other side. Get to know your spirit guides and your personal angels. Learn about our guardian angels.
- Learn a technique for remembering your dreams and about OBEs, or out-of-body experiences, through directed Astral Projection.
- Learn, also, to never fear death. Have you ever wondered why children die? Do they grow up on the other side? Are they the secret playmates of your childhood? Do our pets go to heaven?
- Learn a procedure for Spirit Releasement for those who not only seem possessed, but actually are.
- It is believed that women are right-brained and men are left-brained. Learn about your beta, alpha, and theta brainwave frequencies.

All of this and more is contained in this book and shows how metaphysics can be an exacting and practical science.

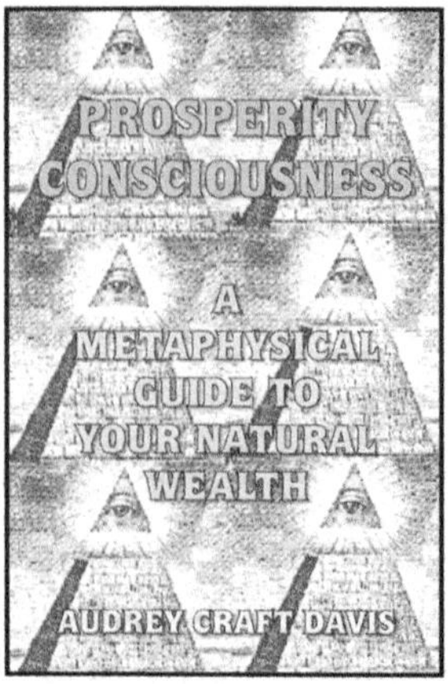

Prosperity Consciousness

A Metaphysical Guide to Your Natural Wealth

Audrey Craft Davis

ISBN: 978-1-57733-203-9, 128 pp., 5.5 x 8.5, paper, $14.95

"It Is Natural to Be Wealthy." God provided enough of everything for everyone on the planet. Begin today to remove the barriers that have kept you from your share. It is costly to be poor and it does no good. Once you attain "prosperity consciousness," you will know it is easier to be wealthy than to give into poverty.

"Your Thought Is a Command." You give permission for every happening in your life by your thought. Once you release a thought, you are responsible for it. It is your offspring.

Never say, *"The Devil Made Me Do It."* Why give the dark forces power over your life? When a minister goes into the pulpit and teaches that the devil is responsible for all poverty, sickness and lack, does he realize he is giving the dark forces the power to inflict pain, illness and poverty? You are responsible for every dark thought you send into God's universe.

"What You See Is What You Get." You cannot think without forming a picture in your mind. When you form a picture, your Angels use it as a grid. This is like a command to them. They were assigned to you to fulfill your wishes. That picture in your mind, good or bad, will happen. Your Angels will see to it!

We are programmed to look for negatives. Watch what happens when you set a goal. Instead of picturing all the good things that can help you succeed, your negative programming takes over and you begin to set up barriers by thinking, "What defenses must I initiate to make sure nothing goes wrong which can keep me from my goal?"

As you can see prosperity consciousness is really a journey into an over-all philosophy of living. It is truly a magnificent journey.

Made in the USA
Monee, IL
19 October 2026

66035053R00075